"Laura is a content m̲ paper. She took my outl̲ was very responsive and patient, and delivered a final manuscript I was very pleased with. We were an Amazon bestseller in my category and have 95%+ 5-star reviews at this point in time. I would recommend Laura and her team to anyone."

— *Jeff Root, owner of SellTermLife & author of 'The Digital Life Insurance Agent'*

"Can I say again how smoothly this process has gone and how happy I am with the manuscript you developed. I'm so grateful that this whole part of the process was completely taken off my hands. Marketing a book is difficult enough without the additional burden of drafting the manuscript, and the fact that I'm so proud of the manuscript (much more so than I would have been if I'd written the whole thing myself) gives me the extra motivation to make the launch as successful as the book deserves."

— *Kiri Masters, owner of Bobsled Marketing Agency & author of 'The Amazon Expansion Plan'*

"The book is better than I had hoped and I can't imagine getting it anywhere near completed without you. Thank you so much for making it a reality, and for capturing and understanding these complex concepts!"

— *Bob Cooper, Jr., owner of El Cheapo Lifts & author of 'Cheap Is Good'*

"Laura—this book wouldn't be possible without your passion and commitment to me and your craft! THANK YOU SO MUCH! I get emotional thinking about how far we've come and I wouldn't have this story so clear without your help."

— *Russ Perry, owner of Design Pickle & author of 'The Sober Entrepreneur' & 'The Creative Entrepreneur'*

"I could not have gotten here without Laura. She had incredible patience, and kept me on the straight and narrow to get this book finished."

— *Brian Kurtz, owner of Titans Marketing & author of 'Overdeliver'*

Published by Gale Creative

Printed in the United States of America

First Printing: 2019

ISBN: 978-1-7337903-0-7

HOW TO WRITE THIS BOOK

Write, Publish & Market Your Business Bestseller

LAURA GALE

Gale Creative

CONTENTS

The life so short, the craft so long to learn.
Geoffrey Chaucer

INTRODUCTION

This book is designed to teach you everything you need to know about writing a book to grow your business. There are plenty of reasons to write a book that pulls back the curtain on your industry, your expertise and your own operation, and as you can see from browsing the business section in any bookshop, or clicking through the business and marketing categories on Amazon, there is a near-endless appetite for this kind of inside information.

Writing a book about your business is effective for a few key reasons:

- It raises the profile of your work, putting you in front of an audience that you might not have been able to reach with your previous marketing efforts.
- It positions you as an authority and expert in your field—if you literally 'write the book' on your industry, you immediately set yourself apart from your competitors.
- It opens up additional revenue streams (like products, courses, and events), bigger and better client projects,

as well as opportunities for media appearances,
speaking engagements and joint ventures.

- It gives you a tangible marketing asset to share with
your audience, potential clients and partners that can
be deployed in diverse and creative ways.
- It is always out there working for you. It doesn't get
sick, or take days off, or change jobs—it's a constant
ambassador for your business and expertise. Every
copy sold serves as a personal sales rep to its reader.

Like any good asset, the value of a book compounds over
time—the initial return, in the form of sales, starts to generate
exponential growth as your readers turn into leads, leads into
first-time buyers, and first-time buyers into loyal, lifelong
customers. As the book gradually earns back more than you
invested in it, it starts to produce a profitable, predictable
revenue stream for your business and brand.

To create a sound investment, you have to go all in. Writing a
great book that defines your place in the industry requires
sharing everything you've learned—all your hard-won experience
and insights, and it requires communicating your deep
understanding of what your market needs in a way that enables
them to make a change.

If you're going to write a successful book, you have to come
at it with a real motivation to help your audience—not just to
make money off them. You have to be willing to share every
detail, every lesson. If you hold back, they'll know... because
they'll try to implement your advice, and it won't work.

That's why this book is specifically written for established
entrepreneurs and business owners. To write a book that is truly
helpful to your readers, you obviously need to know quite a bit
more than your target reader. You will only be able to guide your
readers along their path effectively if you have a proven map of
the territory—proven by having walked it yourself many times.

That's not to say that entrepreneurs early on their journey

don't have valuable information to share—many do—but publishing a book is like throwing accelerant on a fire. Whatever is already happening in your business will be magnified if you follow this process, so it's critical that you're able to meet that increase effectively. Tim Conley, a past client of mine who is an operations consultant from Arizona, lays it out like this:

> Every business will break under pressure. I don't care how many SOPs you have or how 'systems driven' you think you are. When you hit exponential growth, you will have problems you can't even imagine right now.
>
> One way or another, your business will break. If it's a service business, your people will feel overwhelmed. You'll have endless fires to put out, and delivering anything more will be out of the question. Service businesses break quickly: there's a hard cap on what you can produce.
>
> If it's a product business, it will break gradually. Parts in the system will wear out or become too inefficient, and one day will come to a complete stop.
>
> Usually something breaks in operations, and fulfillment is often the first thing to go. You can do all the marketing you want, but if you can't fulfill the demand you're going to have a bad time.
>
> The problem is that if there is any inefficiency in your operation, it will scale at the same rate as the growth. If you have problems when producing 100 units a day, it will be 10 times worse when you're producing 1000 units a day.
>
> Let's say your business currently has 100 customers and you know your systems will break at 1000. What can you change in your systems *now*, so that they could theoretically handle that 1000?[1]

If you are very early in building your business, I would recommend putting this book aside for the moment. If you don't have a proven sales system, and reliable customer service and fulfillment mechanisms, come back to this project when these critical drivers are in place. It's far better to start building a good reputation and developing your customer base—all your resources should be going to developing your audience, honing your offers and learning what kind of creative material they respond to. Focus on finding out what your market really wants, how they want it, and what they'll pay to get it, so that you prove your model, and *then* write your book. It's much easier to write about something that is clearly defined and has been proven over and over again.

And if you're looking for a get-rich-quick scheme, this isn't it. Writing a business book is not the right move for people who need a quick cash injection. Producing content in all forms is a long-term play, and while a book is arguably the most powerful of all content assets and will certainly produce returns, it will likely be a few months before you start making real money off it. Production can take anywhere from three months (if a professional is helping you write and publish the book), to a year or more if you're working on your own. Writing a book can put significant demands on your time, energy, and attention. Most business books have word counts of 30,000 to 70,000 words (roughly 150 to 300 pages), and require a lot of work besides the actual writing (editing, design, publication and marketing, to name a few key parts).

It's also important to keep in mind that writing is a profession in and of itself. Professional writers train for years to become competent and competitive with other professionals in their field, just as you studied and worked for many years to get to where you are now in your own profession. It goes far beyond putting words on a page, which is why so many people have such a hard time ever actually writing the book they have in mind— they don't realize how many additional elements go into producing the final asset beyond just writing the material.

This is why I always remind entrepreneurs and business owners that it's not their fault if they're having a hard time with writing. All their professional development has been focused on building the skills they need to *run* their business, not to write about it. And for most of them, it doesn't make much sense to spend a lot of time honing their writing abilities. (Of course, I believe it serves *everyone* to be able to write well. There's only upside in being able to communicate clearly and engagingly, but there comes a point of diminishing returns in studying the skillset when you are trying to grow or manage a business.)

The quantity a professional writer produces in a day varies a lot, but for most, the average seems to be between 1000 and 3000 words a day. That means that to write a mid-length book, say 50,000 words, you would need to produce 1250 words every working day, without fail, for two months. (In fact, you'll probably need to write about 65,000 to 70,000 words, because editing will often remove at least 20 to 30 percent of the original material.) For context, it took me two hours to get 1500 words down for this book this morning, and this is my second attempt at writing this section, so I'm not even starting from scratch!

There are people in the self-publishing world who would say that the easiest way to overcome these hurdles of time and effort is just to record yourself talking into your phone's voice recorder and have it transcribed into your 'book'. Personally, I think that's rubbish. While recording yourself 'talking the content' can provide a useful foundation to work from when you actually sit down to write, just publishing a collection of transcriptions as a book can do your brand real harm. A transcribed book can be almost impenetrable for readers, and it makes the 'author' look amateur and disorganized.

This is because the way we speak differs significantly from the way we write and read. You might have heard the advice to "write as you speak," but that advice is incomplete if you're trying to produce a quality piece of work. Most people speak in much simpler terms than they write in, and speech is much more forgiving when we ramble, choose less accurate words, or jump back and forth between ideas. In writing, that stream of consciousness becomes very messy, very fast, and that's why just transcribing a conversation or recording is unlikely to produce excellent reading material.

If we are agreed that your book is going to go out into the world as a representative of your business and your expertise, then I think we can also agree that you would want that book to be of the highest quality possible. Would you send a sales rep out on the road looking dishevelled, with only half the sales pitch written and your contact details scribbled on the back of an envelope? No! You would send them out looking immaculate, with a beautiful, complete pitch deck and with a professional, appealing business card, app or website to help customers to take their next steps with your offer.

Remember that you're competing for your reader's most scarce resource: their attention. You are not just competing with the other people in your industry for market share, but with the writers and marketers that work with your competitors too—professionals who communicate and persuade for a living—so it's critical to the success of your book that your material is unique, insightful and polished.

This is why every business owner who wants to write a book owes it to themselves to take the project seriously and to do it right, the first time around. You get just one shot at really impressing your audience with a project like this, and the first part of winning their attention (and business) is demonstrating that you know your industry better than anyone, that you know how to communicate that expertise, and that you care about doing a good job.

WHY LISTEN TO ME?

Well, in the last few years I've written ten books, both working with clients and for my own business.

I have a degree in writing and publishing, and got started in the publishing business as a publicist for Hachette, a global publishing house. I worked on projects like the Twilight phenomenon, JK Rowling's post-Harry Potter publications, and the personal memoirs of Michael Palin, Nelson Mandela and Tina Fey.

I am certified by Digital Marketer in content marketing, conversion funnel optimization, and traffic acquisition, and am a bestselling author myself—my first book, *Content That Converts: How to Build A Profitable and Predictable B2B Content Marketing Strategy* was at the top of Amazon's marketing category for several months.

Ghostwriting is the best way for me to help entrepreneurs and marketers to write, publish and market books that transform their businesses, because I have seen just how powerful books can be, across many different industries. I know how hard business owners work (and how much incredible knowledge is stored up in their heads) so my job is to help entrepreneurs like you to tell your stories, teach your expertise, and increase the impact and growth you can have with your business. But I can't work with everyone, so it's time for me to practice what I preach —to get everything I know about writing out of my head down onto paper, so that knowledge can go out into the world to start helping more people.

CLEARING OUT THE FEARS

Writing a book can be stressful. Exposing every little detail about your business, which you've worked so hard on, and protected so fiercely, feels risky and counterintuitive. Not only do you feel yourself to be under the spotlight of your readers' attention, but you worry about your competitors getting hold of your secret sauce, too.

This is probably the biggest block people bring to the process of writing a book. They're really, really scared of three things:

- That their competitors are going to see what they're doing.
- That they're going to lose the air of mystery that makes clients want to know more.
- That people will stop hiring them (since customers will now be equipped to do it all themselves).

All those fears are understandable. But they're all misplaced, too.

FEAR #1: COMPETITORS

Most of your competitors are unlikely to read your book.

Even if they do, most of them will not have the resources (or inclination) to change their strategy if their approach is very different to yours. Even if they do decide to change their strategy, it's going to take them a long time to catch up to you, and the momentum you will have generated by writing the book will have taken you to a new level anyway. Not only will it take them a long time to catch up, but it's almost impossible that they would be able to recreate the conditions that helped you get established in the first place, or the momentum or opportunities that your particular path has created for you.

FEAR #2: LOSS OF MYSTIQUE

If you are relying on mystery, or are deliberately obscuring your business practices from customers, you need to address that lack of transparency before you write a book.

Why don't you want your customers to understand how you do business? Do you not really know what you're doing? Are you overcharging for the value you provide? Or are you suffering from Imposter Syndrome, and fear the attention and spotlight a book could create for you?

Like I said earlier: a book is an accelerant, and if things are not ship-shape in your business before publication, they will definitely come apart afterwards. This fear is usually rooted in some limiting belief or fear, which requires more therapy than I'm equipped to deliver here.

FEAR #3: THE DIY CUSTOMER

If you think customers will drop you and start doing what you do for themselves... please, let me introduce you to my friend, Inertia.

Inertia is the force that stops people doing the hard things, even when they have all the information to do it. As Derek Sivers, one of the earliest internet business success stories, says: "If information was the answer then we'd all be billionaires with perfect abs."[2]

Most people are going to read your stuff, think "Wow! That's cool, now I totally get it!" Then they will go back to everything on their to-do list and really hope someone will turn up to do everything you just mapped out for them.

(That 'someone' should obviously be you, which is why it's so important to include a strong call to action before the end of the book. This is the primary opportunity of writing a book: you get to demonstrate that you know everything about this area, and that you are the best person to implement it for your readers— more on that later.)

Finally: knowledge protects your customers and allows you to establish better relationships with them. You never want someone to come into an interaction with you blind, without enough insight to judge whether you're being straight with them. The power balance is too much in your favor, and the prospect can feel like you hold all the cards. If they don't have enough information to assess whether you're being honest and transparent with them, it makes people feel defensive, and wary of you trying to 'put it over them'.

Assuming you're being cool—providing value, and not trying to take advantage of your audience—your readers will get to know, like and trust you through reading the book. Their confidence will be boosted by understanding your process, so the dynamic between you becomes more positive and collaborative. You get to build rapport and understanding with them throughout the book, before you ever interact with them personally.

You want to make sure your readers understand everything, so that they have a locus of control in your interactions. Remember: your customers have their own things to do. They *want* someone to take care of the stuff outside their wheelhouse. Understanding your process makes them more comfortable with you and more open to everything you're offering. Your book is the perfect opportunity to hand that confidence and sense of control to them on a silver platter.

And while it might happen occasionally that a potential customer uses your book as a DIY manual, I would argue that those are often not the customers you want to work with anyway. If they are spending time implementing ideas that are not their area of expertise, they are probably very price-sensitive, controlling, early in their business or a combination of all three. That's a pretty stressful client profile, if you ask me, so let them do it themselves. Your ideal clients will read the book, immediately see the value in your process and expertise, and will be happy to let you handle it for them—they'll pay what you ask and then get out of the way to let you do what you do best, while they spend their time doing what *they* do best.

In the following chapters, we'll be delving into exactly how you create that kind of book—the specific workflow and processes I use every time I sit down to write a book, whether for my own business or for my clients. By the end of the book, you'll be able to decide if you want to use this process to write your own book, or whether you want to hand the project off to a partner like me to help you get it done.

For now, it's time to jump into the nuts and bolts of writing your book. The first few chapters are the critical pre-production processes that set your book up to succeed, before you've even written a word. These are the strategic filters that will help you decide if writing a book is right for you and your business, and how to lay the groundwork for the long-term success of the project once you've decided to go ahead.

(I see you, skimmers—don't skip these early chapters. I get that you just want to write the damn thing, but these strategic elements are absolutely foundational and your book will bomb if you don't understand them.)

Once you've laid this groundwork, you'll learn everything you need to produce excellent material and to publish it like a professional. Finally, we'll cover how to market the book in a way that makes it irresistible reading to your ideal clients, and to leverage the momentum from your launch to make it into an evergreen asset for your business. You'll also see some case studies from people I've worked with, as well as a reading list with the books I rely on myself to hone my writing and marketing skills.

By the time you reach the end of the book, you'll have the exact, play-by-play system I use to write and publish multiple books per year for high-end clients, the marketing strategies we roll out to turn the books into bestsellers, and the resources I rely on to make it all as easy and smooth as possible.

Let's get going.

✣ 1 ✣

DEFINING THE PURPOSE OF YOUR BOOK

IN THIS CHAPTER, WE'RE GOING TO EXPLORE THE fundamental purpose of your book—the 'North Star,' or guiding principle, of *why* you are writing it. The North Star is the shining light that will guide you through the entire process of writing, editing, publishing and marketing your book, providing you with a simple, elegant metric against which you can measure every decision:

Does this task or idea help or hinder me in achieving that North Star?

The reason it's so important to define your North Star is that it's very easy to get lost in the weeds when you're working on a book. It happens almost imperceptibly: you strike out boldly in one direction, heading straight on 'til morning, or so you think. A pause here, a misstep there, and suddenly you're completely off course. You might start with a general idea of writing an analysis of your industry so you can impress your audience with your future projections, but soon realize you've focused on microscopic, irrelevant examples. Or you might want to write a history of your company that inspires people to work with you, but find yourself writing character assassinations of your competitors, which would ultimately reflect poorly on your business.

If you haven't defined the specific purpose of the book, often you won't even notice when you're getting off track, until you're so lost that it's easier to scrap all your progress and start again. This happens to writers all the time—and it happened to me, writing this very book. When I started writing for the first time, I had two competing ideas for my North Star, and instead of following my own advice, I tried to 'just start working, and see how they came together'. Wrong, wrong, wrong. I wrote 20,000 words that I discarded altogether because the singular purpose just wasn't clear enough.

(Funnily enough, this phenomenon is borne out by research. A 2009 study by the Max Planck Institute for Biological Cybernetics found that without a specific feature to move towards, people in landmark-free environments, like forests and deserts, end up walking in circles, and very small circles at that.[1] Not only that, but they consistently believe that they are walking completely straight, not realizing that for all their effort, they've made absolutely no progress. It is exactly the same in attempting to write a book without a clearly identified North Star.)

So, how exactly do you define this all-important North Star? By answering a few questions in as much detail as you can possibly manage, and then distilling all that material down into a single sentence that communicates the book's overarching intent.

WHO ARE YOU WRITING FOR?

This is an absolutely critical element in deciding what to write, and how to write it. Businesses exist to serve their customers, and business books are no different. Don't forget that your book is going to be a marketing asset, and that every good marketing campaign starts with a deep and thorough understanding of the customer it is targeting. In fact, this is so important that the next chapter is dedicated entirely to understanding your reader, but if you can answer the preliminary customer profile questions below, you will be able to map out your North Star now, with the option to refine it later if more details come to light once you've done the Reader Avatar deep dive.

BASIC READER AVATAR QUESTIONNAIRE

IS THE READER FOR THIS BOOK:

- A potential client?
- A potential employee?
- Someone who works (or wants to work) in your industry?
- A potential investor?
- An existing investor?
- Something else?

WHAT IS THEIR LEVEL OF KNOWLEDGE OF YOUR INDUSTRY OR BUSINESS?

- They don't know it exists.
- They've heard of it but don't know much about it.
- They know a little bit, enough to be curious.
- They know a fair amount, enough to be dangerous.
- They are an expert.
- Have they consumed any content from you before? If yes: what is the type of content that has been most effective? What is the style they respond to best? What do they come to you specifically to learn, and

what (if anything) have they told you they want more
of? If no: whose content *do* they consume? What is
the style? What might they be hoping to learn
from you?

Note that all these questions are about psychographics, not
demographics. We are looking for what your reader is motivated
by, what they hope for, what they fear—not what age bracket
they fall into or how often they trade in their car. Developing
your reader avatar is about understanding what makes them tick,
deep down, under the surface.

Peter Drucker, one of the most successful business
consultants to ever live, said that "the aim of marketing is to
know and understand the customer so well the product or
service fits him and sells itself."[2]

This is why we need to get to the core of who your reader is
and what they want—so that buying the book, and acting on
what it teaches them, is a foregone conclusion.

WHY YOU? WHY NOW?

These questions—why you, and why now—are distinct, but they
tend to go hand-in-hand. Whether your readers have been in
your audience for years, recently heard you on a podcast, or
picked the book up off a shelf in an airport bookstore,
something specific about you and what you are teaching will
compel them to buy. Often, that is influenced by something
going on in the world (or in *their* world) that makes this
particularly urgent. Uncovering that reason is going to help you
determine everything you write about in this book.

FIRST: WHY YOU?

- Are you known for solving a particular kind of problem?
- Do you have unique experience or insight that no one else can offer?
- Have you had success where others have failed?
- What differentiates you from your competitors?
- What makes your story interesting and informative?
- What will a reader get from your book that they won't be able to get anywhere else?

SECOND: WHY NOW?

- Is there a trend or zeitgeist happening in the marketplace or wider society that makes your message particularly relevant or important?
- Has something changed that is putting pressure on them? If not, is some big change widely expected to happen soon?
- Has something happened in your business that gives you greater leverage in your industry and with your audience to position yourself as an expert?
- Has something happened within your industry that is compelling you to educate the reader in their own best interest?
- Are there external forces in play that mean it's 'now or never' to publish this book?

Finally, it's key to ensure that the book you produce is a logical extension of work you've already done. Brian Kurtz (whose book, *Overdeliver*, was both one of the most rewarding projects I've worked on and a seminal addition to the world's cache of marketing knowledge) has spent nearly 40 years in direct response marketing, and one of his biggest priorities on any campaign is ensuring that the audience recognizes what you're offering them, in relation to everything you've sent them before. He puts it like this:

> Let me quote Will Rogers: "It takes a lifetime to build a good reputation, but you can lose it in a minute."
>
> When you change your voice or allow a different "voice" into the picture you may not only confuse your audience, you could repel them too. And trust can be lost forever... and in a heartbeat.
>
> If you are playing a long game, and I hope you are, never abdicate, even in a small way, who you are and who you want to be in the world; and there is no reciprocation that should ever compromise how you want to treat your best customers... and specifically how you talk to them and interact with them. And that goes for prospects or even suspects (who you eventually want to turn into prospects and then customers)...
>
> Not every marketer needs to be super aggressive nor does every marketer need to be meek... but what you must do is market congruently (and with consistency) so that no one can ever say that you are out of integrity with who you are, what you believe, how you express yourself and what you sell or market.[3]

When you can answer all these questions, you will start to get a feel for what the reader is specifically looking to learn from you, and why. Armed with that knowledge, you can map out the material that is going to be most appealing, insightful, and useful for them.

WHAT'S YOUR USP?

Having a clear USP (unique selling proposition) is a critical element in determining what you write, and how you write it. There is so much material available—online, in books, on podcasts

—that your content needs to be very clearly differentiated in order to cut through all that noise. Perry Marshall, one of today's great marketers, shares the framework for nailing down your USP in this excerpt from his book, *Ultimate Guide to Google Adwords*:

> A USP stands for "unique selling proposition." It's the thing that makes you unique in the marketplace—it's what customers can get from you that they can't find anyplace else.
>
> Having a clear USP gives you a clear response for these questions:
>
> *How are you unique?*
>
> *In what way are you different from your competitors?*
>
> *Why should I buy from you, rather than from someone else?*
>
> *Why should I care at all about you or anything you sell?*
>
> The term came from Rosser Reeves, a pioneer in the use of TV ads. His message on USPs was simple:
>
> Your ad has to have some way of clearly saying, "Buy this product, and you will get this specific benefit."
>
> Your promise has to be one that your competitor cannot or does not offer.
>
> Your promise has to win over new customers.
>
> A USP is worthless if it doesn't convince people to buy from you. USP is the knife-edge of your chisel that empowers you to "chisel your way in" anytime, anywhere. If you're not getting enough traction, sharpen your USP.
>
> Any time you're communicating with a prospect, you can appeal to any one of these, or all of them together:
>
> 1. You're unique because of the buyer you serve.
>
> 2. You're unique because of what you sell.
>
> 3. You're unique because you have an unusual angle.
>
> 4. You're unique because of what your product or service does not do.
>
> 5. You're unique because of the time frame around your offer.

    6. You're unique because of how you guarantee your
product.[4]

Ultimately, this whole chapter on developing your North Star
is about identifying the USP of your book, and simplifying it
until you have a clear one-liner that instantly identifies the
benefit the reader will get from reading it.

(And if you are unclear on the USP of your business overall—
if you can't easily answer the questions above and explain what
makes your business unique—I would suggest that it's more
important to focus on developing that before you tackle writing
a book. When you have proven differentiation from your
competitors and a steady flow of customers coming to you
because of that differentiation, then you're more likely to be ready
to write your book.)

WHAT WILL THE BOOK'S ROLE BE?

As with any marketing asset, your book has to justify its place in
your marketing ecosystem. It's far too big an investment—of
time, money and sheer effort—to write a book that doesn't
generate a significant return for you. As a business owner, you
understand that writing a book that 'sits in the bottom drawer' is
just not an option... it has to be out there, working for you, like
your sales team, like your email funnels, and like your ad
campaigns. It's an active asset, so plan its role in your business
from the start.

    Think about how the book can generate significant new
revenue streams. Yes, if you market it aggressively and
consistently, you can make a reasonable amount of money from
unit sales, but I argue that the real money comes from the flow-
on effect of the book: new clients, greater market share,
speaking engagements, related products and events, and so on.
The book can create momentum and new opportunities that
become the main focus of your marketing long after publication.

For example, most of my ghostwriting clients focus on using their book to generate bigger, better client deals. They use the book to get in the door with clients that were previously out of reach—because now they have published proof that they know what they're doing (and it's also a powerful way to get past gatekeepers who might screen your calls, but will happily pass a book and handwritten note along to your prospect).

Others use the book as the front-end offer that generates an initial sale, but build out an entire suite of back-end offers to generate a second, third, fourth, fifth sale... often creating ten times the revenue from just one of these offers than they made from the initial sale of the book—the book is just the tool that brought the customer in the door.

Still others use their books to start high-ticket mastermind programs, which gives them access to some of the best and brightest minds in their industries, and a willing pool of customers to deal with directly. And many clients do all this and more—with the book as the foundation of the whole system.

SHOULD IT EVEN BE A BOOK?

This might seem like I'm being snarky, but it's an important question to consider before you dive in: do you actually have enough material to justify writing an entire book? Like I said at the start, business books usually have word counts of between 30,000 and 70,000 words. It's not a fixed rule, and there are plenty of exceptions, but if you write 10,000 words, pad out the document with images and tables, and stick it on your website as your 'free book,' you've created a lead magnet, not a book.

There's nothing wrong with lead magnets, but if you're aiming to publish a serious piece of work that advances your business in a meaningful way, writing a glorified blog post is not going to cut it. Your readers, if they are coming to you to learn something specific and important, expect a level of depth and focus that is difficult to achieve if you only write at a surface level. If you start writing and find that you have run out of material at 10,000 words, that's fine—publish and promote it as a long-form article that can be developed into a book later if you want to go deeper. You can still use it to generate podcast interviews, social media coverage and word of mouth marketing, while saving up your 'relationship capital'—the trust and respect readers have for your work that makes them willing to buy—for when you are ready to publish something longer.

SO NOW THAT YOU'VE GONE THROUGH ALL THOSE QUESTIONS, take a minute to write down a first version of your North Star. Remember: you want a clear idea of who you're writing for, what they want to learn from you specifically, and why. Often this exercise is enough to develop a perfectly clear guiding principle for your book, but if you feel the need to refine your idea, come back to this exercise once you've worked through the next few chapters.

✤ 2 ✤

DEFINING YOUR READER

UNDERSTANDING YOUR READER IS THE MOST CRITICAL element of writing your book. I know I said that in the last chapter, and I'm going to keep repeating it—a deep, accurate empathy and insight to your reader's psyche is the most important asset you can have in place when you start writing.

This is because when you write a book with a specific person in mind, the material you include (and exclude) is going to be perfectly tailored to their needs. It's going to answer the questions that are in the front of their mind, *and* the questions they didn't even realize they had. It's going to soothe their fears and empower them to make decisions in their own best interest.

Not only that, but having this level of detail makes it simple for you to find your ideal readers on the various marketing platforms and channels available, to create offers and copy that make buying your book (and acting on what you say) irresistible to them. It allows you to go on to create back-end funnels that lead each customer through offers that are relevant and valuable to them, thereby increasing your customer loyalty and the total lifetime value of each customer.

BUILDING A READER AVATAR

If you're unfamiliar with the concept of creating an avatar (also called a buyer persona), it's the process of defining who your ideal customer is, what they want, what they fear, what they are driven by, what their challenges are, what their opportunities are, and what your opportunities are in serving them. In their Customer Avatar worksheet, which you can find in the footnote below, Digital Marketer calls this exercise 'the Swiss Army Knife of marketing': "Any part of the marketing and sales process that "touches" the customer (which is pretty much EVERYTHING) will improve when you get clear on your customer avatar. After all, it's a person who buys our products and services. It pays to get clear on the characteristics of that person, so you can find and present them with a message that moves them to action."[1]

The purpose behind creating a customer avatar is to develop a deep understanding of the motivations, fears, desires, and problems that influence customer buying decisions. It helps to create a profile that indicates the customer's priorities, goals and challenges, so that you can tailor your positioning and offers to serve them best.

To be clear: you are always going to have multiple types of customers. People are too complex to be categorized down into a single tidy box that predicts all their behaviors. You probably have several types of people who want your services already. Your priority here, though, is to identify your primary customer—the person for whom your product or service is a no-brainer and who will get great returns on their investment with you. More specifically, you are looking to identify your primary *reader*—the person who will get the best results from reading your book and applying the information they find there.

Again, you will most likely have multiple reader avatars, and we'll refer to these as your secondary and tertiary readers. While much of the information will inevitably be applicable to *all* your reader avatars, focusing on your primary avatar gives you two advantages: first, they are the readers most likely to want to work with you afterwards, and are therefore your highest points of leverage with this project, and second, your secondary and tertiary readers will usually find the bulk of what they need within the material directed at the primary reader, so you will simultaneously build up goodwill and credibility with those audience segments too.

In my first book, *Content That Converts*, I covered how to develop a customer avatar for your content marketing efforts that continues to be relevant to that type of marketing today. However, since writing *Content That Converts* (and writing and publishing several other books with clients in the interim), I've realized that the model I used there for developing an avatar is only one of two possible methods.

That model is data-driven, based on the numbers, and very analytical, which works well for the B2B companies I was writing for at that time, but as I've worked with more consultants, coaches and creative entrepreneurs, another methodology has emerged—intuitively modeling the avatar on an actual person. I call these the Analytical Model and the Relational Model respectively.

Where the avatar profile in the original Analytical Model is developed by answering dozens of questions, analyzing analytics and sales data, and surveying existing and potential customers, the profile for the Relational Model is built around a specific person. For example, when Molly Pittman and I kicked off work on her book, she already had a clear idea of who her primary readers were—and they were people she knew personally. Her book was about the revolution of digital work, with a particular focus on teaching media buying as a powerful and valuable career for anyone who wanted to have more autonomy and fulfillment in their work, greater control over their income, and a future-proof skillset. Of course, with her background in media buying, Molly has an exceptional gift for identifying and analyzing critical data, so she had plenty of hard facts to support her

Relational Profiles, but she was primarily focused on serving people similar to those she had interacted with personally.

Her first avatar was a friend working in a corporate role, grinding away for long hours every week, feeling bored and unfulfilled in his work, who was looking for a new opportunity. Another friend who had worked in start-ups was in the process of launching an e-commerce store, and desperately needed traffic and predictable revenue to make her new venture work. Molly's third avatar was her young cousin, who went to college on a football scholarship but knew that what he was learning would be redundant in a few years and was looking for ways to ensure his skills would be competitive for the duration of his working life.

So there are two ways of working through this section, and you'll probably have a reflexive sense of which approach is right for you: data driven and analytical, or intuitive and relational (and of course, pairing the two options together is a good way to ensure that your avatar is as clear and reliable as possible).

HOW TO BUILD AN ANALYTICAL MODEL

If you're using the data-driven model, the following section, taken from *Content That Converts*, provides a framework for you to build on. Where the relational model is based on people you actually know, the analytical model is based on what you believe you know about people in your audience. Once you've got this as your foundation, we'll move on to the specific, tactical steps of building out your avatar (but keep in mind that, like any good science experiment, this model requires that you test your hypothesis before you start building a whole project around it):

The Harvard Business Review recommends a three-fold approach to identifying if a market segment is right for your business: perspective, capabilities and profit potential.

Assessing perspective is about making sure the customer's attitudes fit with yours. You want to make sure that they have similar priorities, sensibilities and and direction to you.

For example, Apple is renowned for its total obsession with design and usability. Their customers are also highly attentive to design and experience, so Apple's product and marketing teams know exactly who get their products in front of. Amazon is relentless in its focus on providing amazing shopping experiences, and so they attract customers who prioritize great service and convenience. The perspectives between the business and the customer are aligned.

Assessing for capabilities is about the 'embedded resources' of your company. These are the assets and resources that position your business to serve one type of customer better than another.

For example, your business might have really strong or innovative technology, highly visible brand equity and marketing, or industry-specific capabilities that other companies have trouble competing with. Any one of those elements make your business much more valuable to a particular type of customer over others. Determining whether your capabilities fit with the perspective and profit potential is key to choosing the right audience.

Last but certainly not least is assessing the profit potential of your chosen market. Do they have budgets that will accommodate your prices? Is your service likely to bring them a sufficiently significant return that it's a no-brainer for them to work with you? Is there enough growth potential in their businesses for you to raise your prices and maintain them as paying customers? Are there other things they need that you can add to your services in order to increase your profit margins?[2]

Writing a book—all of marketing, really, and in fact all of business—is about people. It's about serving your audience, caring deeply about their problems, and using your expertise and experience to help them solve those problems.

It's impossible to write a meaningful, effective book without interacting with your audience. You *must* be willing to speak with them, to ask what they want to know, to hear what it is they *really* need—not what you think they need—before you start writing. You can do all the data analysis you want, but without understanding who they are and what they are motivated by, you won't write the book they need to read.

So if you are going to rely on an analytical model, you will also need to survey actual people to confirm that your profiles are accurate. I recommend using the 'Ask' survey structure built by Ryan Levesque, in his book of the same name, and we'll cover a lot of the relevant questions in the psychographic and demographic questions for this model below.

PSYCHOGRAPHIC QUESTIONS

As you go through these questions, answer each of them for your avatar, in regard to both their personal and professional lives. Even though you are intending to write a business book, keep in mind that for many people, their professional lives are extensively influenced by their personal lives. Assume that your readers are not great at compartmentalizing these different spheres of their lives, and that if they are having personal challenges, their professional lives will be affected, and vice versa.

WHAT ARE YOUR READER'S GOALS?

- How do they want to feel? How do they want to be perceived?
- What do they want to achieve?
- What are their values?
- What do they believe about themselves?
- What do they believe about themselves in relation to other people? Do they have imposter syndrome or do they secretly think they're better than everyone else, or is it somewhere in between?

- Are they motivated by legacy, freedom, fame, or wealth?
- What are the pressures they are facing day-to-day?

What's changing in their industry?

- What's happening in their specific role?
- Are they being affected by their health, family or social situation?
- What are the limitations they are facing day-to-day?
- Do they have tiny budgets to work with, or difficult teams?
- Do they have too many responsibilities, or not enough?
- Are they being asked to do the impossible, or do they have so few limitations that they're paralyzed by indecision?

Who are they influenced by?

- Industry leaders?
- Media figures or public personas (ie podcast hosts, TV hosts, writers etc)?
- Personal relationships (partner, friends, children)?
- Professional relationships (peers, bosses, mentors, teams)?

What do they believe is necessary to success?

- Do they believe in the 'hustle' mentality of business-building? Or do they believe in seasonal cycles of work and rest?
- What do they believe would cause them to immediately fail at their chosen pursuit? What would make them immediately succeed?

- Would this occurrence actually make them fail or succeed? If not, why do they believe this?

Demographic Questions

- How old are they?
- How does this influence their attitudes?
- Where do they live?
- Does this influence their world view, politics, personal values?
- What is their job title?
- Do they have the power to make decisions about the direction of their work? Or are they reliant on someone else's decisions?
- What is their sociocultural and socioeconomic position?
- Are they married or in a partnership? Do they have children? Do they live alone, with a nuclear family unit, in a blended family or in a multi-generational situation?
- Are they financially secure? If so, are they wealthy? If not, are they poor? How does their financial position affect their self-perception and actions?
- What is their level of education?
- How does this affect their self-perception and actions?
- What is their political orientation?
- Does this affect them professionally or personally? If so, how?
- How do they like to receive their information?
- Online:
- Podcasts
- Online news outlets
- Social media
- Email lists

- Offline:
- Newspapers
- Magazines
- Books
- TV
- Radio

HOW TO BUILD A RELATIONAL MODEL

Now, if you can think of a specific person or specific people that you want to write for, I suggest writing out a profile of them. Write about them in detail, drawing on everything you personally know about that person:

- Who are they? What is their current situation?
- What is their big problem?
- Is the problem they *think* they have the problem they *really* have?
- Is this a real-world problem (something that is happening in the physical world) or an inner-world problem (something that is happening mentally or emotionally)?
- What is their motivation for solving that problem?
- What will it mean for them personally to have moved past their problem—how will their life be different as a result?
- Will they make more money? Be more relaxed? Have more time? Feel more confident about the future? Receive more recognition? Experience more fulfillment?
- What are they afraid of when they think about this part of their life?
- Are they scared they will run out of money and become destitute?

- Are they scared they will be perceived as a failure, and become an outcast in their community?
- Are they scared they will never achieve something with their life, and be forgotten?
- What are the limitations they put on themselves when they think about trying to solve this problem?
- Do they doubt they are smart enough, technical enough, rich enough, sexy enough to do it?
- Do they have models of people they can relate to who have solved this same problem?
- Do they even truly believe it's possible to achieve their goal or solve their problem?

Once you've mapped out these profiles of your reader avatars, go back to your North Star: is the overarching theme and idea for your book still the right material to produce for your primary reader? If not, work through the North Star exercises again until you're satisfied that you have the right guiding principle mapped out for your book. And if you feel that you got it right the first time, can you refine the idea any more, now that you have a better understanding of who your audience will be?

LEVELS OF AWARENESS AND SOPHISTICATION

Another element in developing a thorough reader avatar, regardless of the model you use, is understanding the level of awareness and sophistication they have about your offer and your industry. This concept comes from *Breakthrough Advertising*, by Eugene Schwartz.

To identify the levels of awareness and sophistication in your audience, you first have to have a clear grasp of what Schwartz calls the 'mass desire' that creates this market:

It is the public spread of a private want... it is the moment when a private desire is shared by a statistically significant number of people, large enough to profitably repay selling to these people, that a market is born. This market may consist of a desire shared by only a few thousand people, such as the urge to own fine antiques. Or it may be shared by tens of millions, as the desire to lose weight. But it is there, demanding to be satisfied, waiting only for the information that will direct it onto a particular product.

Once you are clear, then, on the Mass Desire that forms the foundation of your market, it's time to identify the level of awareness your prospect has of this desire in themselves. Schwartz continues:

How much aware is that prospect of that desire? How close is it to the surface of his consciousness? Is he aware only that a problem or need exists, or is he aware if they can be satisfied? And if he is aware that a means of satisfaction exists, does he realize that it lies in your group of products, or specifically in your product by name, or more specifically in your product at a given price?[3]

LEVELS OF CUSTOMER AWARENESS

Let's work through the levels of awareness so you can easily map out this data about your readers, as their level of awareness will dictate the type of information you need to include:

COMPLETELY UNAWARE

The prospect has not yet recognized (or admitted) to themselves that they have a problem, and their need is so undefined in their minds that it's difficult to summarize or even verbalize.

. . .

NEED AWARE

The prospect recognizes that they have a need but hasn't yet become sufficiently motivated to solve it, or they don't realize that there is a connection between your solution and the fact that they could solve that need.

DESIRE AWARE

The prospect knows that they have a problem and that they want a solution, but they don't know yet that there is an offer in the market—your offer—that will do what they want.

SOLUTION AWARE

The prospect knows that there is a solution in the market to their problem, but doesn't yet know about your product specifically, or doesn't yet believe that it is the best option for them. The majority of prospects in business niches fall into this category.

PRODUCT AWARE

The prospect knows about your product, knows what it does, and knows that they want it, because they believe it will meet their desire or solve their problem.

LEVELS OF MARKET SOPHISTICATION

Where the levels of awareness are about the customer's degree of identification of their own problem and the solutions available to them, levels of market sophistication are about the range of solutions they have been exposed to as a group (and the promises that have been made to them).

The levels of market sophistication could also be described as levels of market cynicism—basically, what the market is willing to believe about a particular type of product, which is largely dependent on how long they have been exposed to solutions to the mass desire in question.

STAGE ONE

This happens when you are first to market with a new type of product. There is virtually no market sophistication, so in this instance, you can basically just say what your solution does, and all the prospects who are Need Aware and Desire Aware are likely to jump at the chance to try it. (This is what happened when Uber arrived on the transport scene a few years ago. Having a personal driver was a pipe dream for most people—until it suddenly wasn't. It solved a huge desire in the market and now all five levels of awareness in the market have been impacted.)

STAGE TWO

The market knows that there is a solution to their problem, so each provider in the market enlarges their claims and pushes the market to believe bigger, better things about the offer. As this stage evolves, the market's level of sophistication moves from a basic level to a more cynical view, due to the ever-increasing promises they are hearing.

STAGE THREE

At this stage, the market has become jaded about all the claims they've heard, and generally believes that all solutions are more or less the same. But the mass desire continues to exert itself and drives people to seek out novel solutions. The only thing that the market responds to at this stage is a fresh mechanism that makes the claims credible again This is where the emphasis in advertising shifts to *how* a product works, rather than just what it *does*.

STAGE FOUR

This fourth stage usually passes quickly. Once the shift of the third stage has happened, every provider in the market piles on to the 'how' mechanism, making claims about their solution doing it faster, easier, more reliably, and soon you're back to having a cynical audience. Long-established markets often loop through this stage many times as different providers come up with different embellishments or mechanisms to keep the audience interested.

STAGE FIVE

This final stage occurs when the messaging shifts to have the audience identify themselves with the product—what does their choice of this product say about them as a person? This is where Uber (and the various other rideshare services that piled on in Stage Two and Three of this process) are at the time of writing: you choose Uber because you are an efficient person who values expediency, or believes in free markets. Or if you take a Lyft, or use Taxify, maybe it's because you don't want to be identified with the controversy that has surrounded Uber. Your choice of share transport says something about your values and beliefs, and so each company's marketing doesn't even have to say what the product does anymore; they can just appeal to the customer's worldview.

IF YOU'RE FIRST TO MARKET, YOU HAVE A HUGE ADVANTAGE, because you're starting with Stage One market sophistication—but most of us are not first to market. Usually, we're just one of many providers in a niche, and so it pays to understand, from a macro perspective, where your specific audience is at, both in terms of their level of awareness and in their level of sophistication.

CREATING NEGATIVE AVATARS

By now, you should have a clear model of who you want to serve, with a clear idea of what they are motivated by, what they fear and what they respond to. But let's be honest—the world has a way of throwing curve balls into even the neatest plans, and nowhere is this more obvious than in business. You can have your plan laid out to perfection, and then a prospect will come along who doesn't fit into any of the categories you've defined. Sometimes that works out, and you end up with a new model for another type of customer you want to serve. And sometimes it goes to hell in a handbasket, and you regret the moment you ever decided to work with that person.

This is why I recommend building out a negative avatar, too —a profile of the person you *don't* want to work with and for whom you are *not* writing. Again, you might have a specific person in mind from a past experience. This profile is not so much about things you didn't like about them personally (though maybe that's a factor), but about the red flags you have noticed in hindsight. These might be things like price sensitivity, attitude to the market or your service, ambivalence about timelines or deliverables, unreasonable expectations of customized services, high churn among their internal team, lack of responsiveness to communications and so on.

How To Identify Your Negative Avatar

- What market segment are they in? Is there something about that segment that doesn't appeal to you or fit with the rest of your model?

- If the problem is with the specific person, what is the behavior that isn't a good fit for you?
- What language do they use or attitudes do they express that make you uncomfortable, confused or apprehensive?
- What are the goals or motivations that don't fit with your offer or attitude?
- Who do they *not* pay attention to? Who or what do they avoid when seeking information?
- What are their objections to your offer? What do they want to do differently to your ideal avatar?

You can never perfectly insure yourself against attracting the wrong audience, but having a clear understanding of who you *don't* want to work with goes a long way to filtering them out automatically.

I know that this chapter has taken a very deep dive into developing your reader avatar, maybe to a level of detail you don't think is necessary. It's easy to just run head first into writing a book you think the market will respond to, or that you are just interested in writing yourself, but ultimately, your reader is the determining factor in whether your book will be a success —whether all the time, effort and resources you put into creating and marketing the book will pay off for you. So even if it seems like overkill to do all this profiling, I encourage you to stick with it, to build up that intrinsic level of empathy and understanding, and to keep your reader front of mind throughout the entire process of producing your book.

❧ 3 ❧

DEFINING THE STRUCTURE OF YOUR BOOK

THERE ARE ALWAYS GOING TO BE VARIATIONS IN HOW PEOPLE develop the structure for their books, but if you can follow a systematic process, it's going to make it much, much easier for you to start actually writing.

The reason that most people get writer's block is that they haven't planned their book sufficiently, and haven't mapped out in enough detail what they want to talk about. Just about anyone who has done any amount of writing has faced this at one point or another—you sit down all motivated to write, coffee at the ready and document open. A few minutes later you realize you're staring at a blank page, or that you've been scrolling through social media without even noticing you switched tabs.

Building up a detailed outline saves you from that vague sense of knowing roughly what you want to talk about, without having a clear hook to get you started. You can think of creating the structure of the book in advance as building the scaffolding that will allow you to build the entire structure.

Too often, would-be writers start work on their big idea, putting words down as they come, and they end up writing themselves into a corner. They get stuck, not being able to fully explain what they want to communicate. They haven't laid the necessary groundwork early on, and realize that they need to backtrack, or explain something out of context, or they have stories and examples wedged in where they don't belong, and it becomes a tangled, chaotic mess that eventually demands completely starting over.

That is obviously extremely frustrating, and a huge waste, which can usually be avoided if the writer maps out what they want to say in a cohesive, structurally sound way. You would never build a house without an architectural plan that you trust, and it's the same thing when you start writing a book.

This is simply about setting yourself up to have the best chance of success possible. When you have a lot of detail to work from right from the start, you make the writing *much* easier on yourself. Give yourself something tangible you can climb up each day in your writing, and ensure that the reader develops a thorough understanding of the concepts you're trying to teach them.

Putting a lot of detail into your outline also saves you from missing critical parts of the puzzle. When you first map out your outline, you'll put down all the obvious ideas and information, but when you come back to look at it again later, you'll notice all kinds of things that were left out—when you take a step back, you can immediately see where your scaffolding is missing critical crossbeams and footholds.

This process works regardless of whether you are writing something very tangible and tactical, or something very conceptual or strategic. When your book is technical, it's generally going to be a pretty linear process to map out everything you need to cover, while the material might not be as obvious with a more strategic or conceptual book. This is the core of the writer's role—to identify and build out the structure and depth that will help the reader really understand the concepts.

If you're writing a theoretical book, the critical element is to make sure that the reader has the same shared foundation of knowledge that you have. If you just assume that your reader understands what you're talking about, you can leave people behind very easily. Remember that we're talking about writing about niche topics within a specific industry or business, where there's often no standard level of education or experience. You can very easily lose people who don't have the same business background as you, and who have potentially never heard of the concepts you take for granted.

I see this with the entrepreneurs I work with all the time. We'll be building out the structure for their book and they will completely gloss over a whole skillset, because it seems so basic to them that they can't see why anyone would be interested in hearing about it. But that 'basic' knowledge might lay a critical foundation for the rest of the information they will be exploring throughout the book. The entrepreneur assumes that everybody must have the same knowledge that they do, and have been so immersed in their particular world for so long that they don't realize how valuable their insights are to people without their experience. I believe that this is why many entrepreneurs and creatives struggle to define their USP or to reach a tipping point in achieving the success they dream of—they minimize or discount their unique abilities and market position. What seems so common and standard to one person can be a revelation to someone else, so even if there are people in your readership who do have a base understanding, it's always worth setting some space aside to recap the foundational material.

THE FIRST PASS

Something to keep in mind when you start working on your outline is that it's going to be a living document. It's going to evolve and grow over time, as you develop more clarity about the project and start to work through each section. Your outline will undergo many, many changes, and that's perfectly fine. Admittedly, you can't keep changing it indefinitely—at some stage you just have to trust that you've included everything that needs to be covered—but when you start out, expect that you will want to add things, fiddle with the order and revise various parts.

When you begin working on your outline, start with the end in mind. What is it that you want the reader to have absorbed when they finish reading this book? What do they need to learn along the way to get to that point? What do you need to convince them of? What evidence do you need to share to bring them to that understanding?

So the first thing you want to do is to brainstorm all the big ideas that you want to cover in your book. Normally I aim for a minimum of ten key concepts, up to about fifteen or twenty, depending on how much material you plan to cover. These concepts will become your chapter topics, and at this stage, they don't need to be detailed—just make a note of the key idea. For example, when I started work on this book, I put down the following concepts as the overarching ideas that I wanted to form the chapters:

- Whether or not writing a book is right for the reader.
- How to define the purpose of the book.
- How to define the reader of the book.
- How to build the structure.
- How to write the draft.
- The multiple stages of editing.
- How to market the book (and when).
- Creating the title and cover design.
- Formatting and publication.
- Launch strategies.
- Ongoing use of the book .
- Case studies.

As you can see, there are twelve topics there, and they roughly form the basis of the book you are reading now. These are big, complex topics with many moving parts and details that I can delve into throughout each chapter.

Once you've got your chapter topics listed out, you go through the list and start adding sub-topics to each point. Add five to ten sub-topics—these will become the sections of each chapter to work through and will provide the key points you will specifically write about. You don't need me to map that out for every single chapter outlined above, but here's one to demonstrate what I mean:

- **How to market the book (and when):**
- Create dream list of features
- Build your community
- Start SEO research
- Outline paid ad strategy
- Develop email list and strategy
- Plan requests of your personal relationships
- Map out your pre-launch campaign

Then you chunk down even further, and start adding specific points to cover when you sit down to write each section:

- **Create dream list of features:**
- Podcasts
- Blogs
- Traditional media
- **Build your community & email list**
- Facebook group/email list
- Ask for feedback on topics
- Share draft material
- Involve them in title and cover design choices
- Ask for early readers
- Create pre-launch activities and competitions
- **SEO research**
- Keyword research

- Category research
- Competition in the niche
- Any obvious opportunities
- **Paid ad strategy**
- Interview (Molly)
- **Personal relationships**
- Hand outreach to join community
- Hand outreach to participate in launch
- Ask for introductions and recommendations
- **Pre-launch campaign**
- Pre-orders
- Social media seeding
- Review commitments
- Email and social copy for promotional partners

You can also make note of whether you want to include a foreword or introduction (written by someone else—usually a visible or influential person in your industry), and where you could include interviews or case studies with other people who could then help you promote the book later on.

As you can see, this becomes quite specific and takes all the ambiguity out of what you would focus on writing each time you sit down to work on the book. There are notes about interviewing people in the industry—always a good way to add credibility and to build in natural promotional partners—and you can include anecdotes or examples to demonstrate an idea as well. It's a good idea at this point to have someone else from your industry (say, a business partner or mentor) look over the outline to make sure you haven't forgotten anything, and to add interesting suggestions and stories from their perspective.

The good thing with this structure is that it takes the big, undefined idea of 'writing a book' and breaks it down into very manageable pieces. You work backwards from your general overarching idea, and at each stage, define more and more detail until you basically have a 'join the dots' puzzle to work on each day.

Keep in mind, too, that the content you include does not have to be brand new. Material you have published before—on a blog, podcast or channel—can be put to good use here with some diligent reworking. Taylor Pearson, author of *The End of Jobs*, put it to me like this:

> I had written a blog for a couple of years prior to starting on my book, so I had a track record and an audience. I felt that a book would be a 'social object', in a way that online content is not. It's something your audience can physically hold and pass around. Books have a history—they've been around for six hundred years, they have a certain weight to them—so even though most of the content of the book had been published on my site previously, the impact of the book was made much greater by the act of converting it into that more valuable format.

DEFINING A CALL TO ACTION

A call to action (CTA) is how you ask your reader to take a next step with you, once they've finished reading the book. For example, if the strategic purpose of the book is to generate leads for your core service, your CTA might be along the lines of, "If you've gotten direction and valuable insights from reading this book, then I'd like to invite you to head over to www.mywebsite. com/video and download the video series we made for you that will teach you exactly how to implement everything you've learned."

Having a clear CTA means that you generate a way to contact your readers after they've gotten to know you, which means you can gradually ascend them through your product line with direct marketing. This is an opportunity to actively put the book to work for you, rather than just waiting for people to take action on their own after reading it (and most people need a specific prompt to make them take that next step, so this is a very important thing to include).

Lindsay Marder, former managing editor of Digital Marketer's content team, and co-founder of Digital Strategy Bootcamps, shared some insights with me on what makes an effective CTA:

> You want to make it really easy and comfortable for someone to opt-in to the next stage of your funnel (or whatever the next logical step in their journey with you will be). If your CTA tells them to book a call with you, or to buy something right away, a lot of people are going to feel intimidated, or they're going to talk themselves out of it because they don't feel like they're ready to make that level of commitment. Commitment is built up really slowly for most people, so you want to make an offer that's just a little bit bigger than what they've already done— they've bought your book and read it, so you know they're definitely interested in what you're teaching, so now the next best thing might be to have them follow you on social media, to try to get an email address with a download or some gated content, or to invite them to something where they're not under a big spotlight, like a private Facebook group or a pre-recorded webinar.

You can mention your CTA a few times throughout the book, wherever you find a natural, congruent place to include it. It should definitely be included at the end of the book, in the conclusion, so that it's the last thing the reader absorbs from the book.

WHY THIS WORKS

If all this structure-building seems prescriptive to you, that's fair enough. But countless books never get written because the author doesn't know exactly what they're going to work on at various stages of the project, and it robs their audience of the expertise and insight that could make all the difference in their businesses.

You might have a negative instinctive reaction to being told what to do in such detail, and I get that—you didn't become an entrepreneur because you like following rules—but if you've never written a book before, try to think of this process as your playbook, rather than your rulebook. Once you know what works, you can adapt the process to your own style as much as you like. But for your first book or two, use this structure to ensure you get the hang of it and can internalize what needs to happen to create a world-class book.

If you don't have enough chapter topics—or you have too many—spend some time investigating what your audience really wants from you. In the previous chapter we did that deep dive into determining who your reader avatar is, and if you have a clear understanding of who your readers are, that should provide the foundational idea for the kind of book you'll write.

If your audience is looking to you for technical know-how—maybe you're the best in the world at building and distributing a particular type of product—then they're going to want that tactical, step-by-step material.

If you're a thought leader or you're trying to transform an industry in some way, or something controversial happened in your business or industry and you're capitalizing on the momentum around that, then the reader is going to want your opinions, your concepts and your unique reactions and insights.

Or if you have been very successful at building businesses, and you're talking about the strategic mindset behind that process for readers who are fairly experienced, then those people probably want to understand how you're managing your relationships, how you manage your time, how to lead effectively, how to build a healthy culture and so on.

What you choose to write about is really a question of what

people are trying to understand from you and why you're uniquely positioned to teach it to them. It's about understanding who your reader is, what they're motivated by and why they are receptive to your opinions.

(And if you still can't put down enough ideas that would be useful to your audience, again, maybe this idea would work better as a long-form article, podcast or video.)

Of course, there's an exception to using this kind of structure too. If you're writing an investigative book—where you set out to solve a problem you don't yet know the answer to, maybe something that's industry-wide or you're looking at future trends —then your structure is going to be more reliant on the questions you need to ask. But the essential idea still holds: build a structure around specific topics and then fill in the data as you find it.

SHOULD YOU LEAD WITH PERSONAL CONTENT OR BUSINESS PRINCIPLES?

A question that occasionally comes up in this kind of project is whether you should rely on your personal story to lead the narrative, or whether you should lead with the principles you are trying to teach the reader, and as is so often the case, the answer is that it depends.

It's really a question of whether your business is personality-driven or not—are you the face of the company? If so, then maybe it makes sense to lead with your personal story; that needs to be a central component of the material, because an interest in *you* will often be the reason a reader has picked up the book. They want to know about you specifically because you have had an interesting journey, your business is very unique or there's some key differentiating factor in your story.

However, a lot of people are not the face of their company. Many entrepreneurs are very motivated to stay out of the limelight—maybe they are interested in selling their company, they really value their privacy, or it's simply not the kind of business that lends itself to being personality-driven. If that's the case and you've determined that your industry would still really benefit from a book from you, then maybe you focus more on the principles and third-person accounts of how things unfolded for your company.

In that scenario, you can personalize the image of that business by including stories of the 'unknown' people behind the scenes. Let's say, for example, that Ford decided to write a book for their next big anniversary. Maybe they would highlight an engineer or an administrator who quietly did something really innovative that could have a profound impact on how the reader does business themselves. Or the book could feature specific employees in each chapter as relevant, getting quotes and ideas from them to weave some human interest throughout. A human element is helpful in making the material relatable for readers, so try to include it whenever possible. Obviously nothing happens in a vacuum and *someone* is making decisions and taking action to drive the business forward, so you have an opportunity to introduce the people behind the scenes as a way of engaging the reader more deeply.

Another key element in creating that human interest in your writing is being transparent and honest. When you're thinking about your structure, don't skim over the failures, mistakes and problems in your journey, even if you're not leading with your personal story. There's something very disarming about being upfront about where things have gone wrong—it makes you relatable because everybody has made mistakes in their own businesses. Including those moments in your story can demonstrate that you're honest and have integrity, that you can identify when you've gotten lucky, and that you have the humility to address the areas where you're still learning or improving.

Not only does it make you seem more trustworthy to people who might be considering working with you, but it also makes for very compelling reading material. Entrepreneurs love an underdog story, and the stories of great comebacks after failure, so if you've overcome a lot of problems, you have a unique opportunity here to step into the role of a mentor. You get to help your readers sidestep the mistakes and failures you experienced. It makes it okay for your readers to acknowledge where they themselves are failing, and there's nothing more important for business owners, entrepreneurs and creatives than to be really honest with themselves. In a business environment like the one we have today, particularly online—where everybody only shares their 'highlight reels' and acts like everything is amazing all the time—it's a huge relief to find out that someone else has struggled too.

Normalizing failure, showing that it's not the end of your business or your career, can be very reassuring to your reader and will help bond them to you more effectively. That's not to say that we should be encouraging or dismissing failure as unimportant, but simply acknowledging that it happens and that with the right attitude and resources, you can get back up and keep going.

❧ 4 ❧

WRITING YOUR DRAFT

ONCE YOU HAVE BUILT OUT YOUR NORTH STAR, YOUR READER avatar and your structure, it's time to actually sit down and start writing. A lot of people come to this point and feel like they are grinding to a halt—usually because they haven't gone through those previous three steps thoroughly enough. If that's you, and you still feel unsure about what you should be writing, or for whom, go back to the exercises in the previous chapters and delve into more detail to give yourself some more clarity and concrete direction.

If you do feel ready, and you're itching to get going, the next step is very simple: just start. Set yourself a time goal or word count goal and write until you're done for the day. Do the same thing tomorrow, and the day after, and keep going until the draft is done.

Don't expect everything to come out right the first time around; it won't. But starting is the first step towards *making* it come out right. There are going to be a few rounds of going through this material that will gradually hone it down into a final product that you're really happy with, so remember that the point of this stage is just to get all of the material out of your head and onto the page.

If you look at the writing habits of famous authors, you will find that they all follow completely different processes for this part. Some write in a stream of consciousness all morning and then revise what they wrote in the afternoon or the next day. Some work line by line, making each sentence say exactly what they want before going on to the next one. Some aim for specific word counts each day; others aim to write consistently for a specific period of time.

There are as many different ways to do this as there are authors, and instead of trying to follow someone else's method, this will likely go easier for you if you let yourself settle into the rhythm that emerges naturally for you. But no matter your working style, this process is a lot like exercise. It can feel like a bit of a grind when you start out, especially if you're not in the habit. And just like exercise, you will need to get warmed up first. Often the first few lines are going to be really tough to get out of your head, and often they will be rubbish. Don't worry about that; it's totally normal. Once you're on a roll, you can change or delete anything that's no good.

GETTING IN FLOW

A lot of professional writers do warm-up exercises, and so do professional artists. Getting in flow comes with practice, so give yourself a little bit of space to get warmed up. The aim is to get yourself in a zone where the words are flowing out of you, your thoughts are coming quickly and clearly, and it's feeling easy for you to follow the structure as you've built it. So if you find yourself struggling to make a start, then write about stuff that's completely unrelated to the book, just to get the gears turning. It might sound like a waste of time, but it works—write about the room you're in, how you're feeling today, what you've been working on recently. Making a start, no matter what you're writing about, will help kick you out of the distractions of the day and into the practice of writing.

And like exercise, the more you write, the easier it gets. The more you write, the more confident you become in your own thoughts, and the faster you can put them down clearly and concisely. So if it's feeling really hard at the beginning, don't get discouraged. It doesn't mean that you're never going to be able to do it. It just means that you're not really in the practice yet. And the more frequently you sit down and work towards particular milestones—finishing a paragraph, a page, a chapter—the easier it's going to get over time.

Time is a critical factor in getting into flow with writing, and you've probably experienced this in developing your own business: it can take a while to get into deep work. Cal Newport defines deep work as "the ability to focus without distraction on a cognitively demanding task. It's a skill that allows you to quickly master complicated information and produce better results in less time."[1] This is not something that happens in fifteen or twenty minutes snatched out of your schedule when you can find it; it happens when you specifically plan for it and protect that time. When we get in flow, most people will spend a few hours immersed in what they're doing. I can usually stay in flow for three or four hours when writing, which means I can consistently produce a few thousand words each day. Now, I know that not everyone has that kind of time—after all, writing *is* my business, so I can afford to put those hours into it every day. You might only have an hour a day where you can focus on this, and that's perfectly fine. You can do deep work in one hour and produce a meaningful amount of content—you just have to protect that time ferociously.

Set aside specific blocks of time in your schedule where you are completely disconnected from everything that could break your focus (you can even put it in your calendar if that will protect the time more effectively). Set your phone to Do Not Disturb or airplane mode and put it in another room. Disconnect your computer from the Internet, or, if you *must* stay connected to do research while you're writing, shut all your tabs.

I know you've probably got about fifteen tabs open right now 'to look at later', but that is an avalanche of distraction ready to come crashing down on your writing time. Save the links if you need to, but shut them down. Shut your apps, too. If you are getting pinged with notifications through Slack or Messenger or WhatsApp or Twitter or any of the millions of other potential distractions, you will not get in flow and you will waste your precious hour.

WRITING RITUALS

If it helps, build up a little ritual to signify to yourself that it's time to write. That might be sitting down in a different place to where you do the rest of your work, lighting a candle, putting on some particular music, or even leaving your workspace for a walk around the block and then coming straight in to sit down and start writing. Develop small habits that help you get in the zone —but don't let yourself end up being controlled by them. In her excellent book *The Forest for the Trees*, famed editor Betsy Lerner advises against allowing these rituals to become so important that you prevent yourself from writing if you can't do them:

> People who write tend to develop a set of ritualized behaviors with regard to their work. These habits dictate when, where, and under what circumstances they feel able to produce. There are early birds and night owls. Some need a bright café to compose. Others must steal away to a secluded spot or the equivalent of a safe house where no one knows their identity. Most require solitude... If you become successful as a writer, these ritualistic behaviors will become known as your "process"... Should you fail to achieve success, all these behaviors look only like excuses or sick behavior.[2]

While I think that for most people, little writing habits can be very powerful psychological switches, that take us from where we are starting to where we need to be, Lerner's final point here is critical to keep in mind: "Every time you put a provision on the conditions under which you can work... you fail to grasp the essential truth of all great writing: it brooks no provisions."

YOUR DAILY MILESTONE

Another way to maximize your momentum is to set yourself a specific milestone to achieve each day. Whether that's a word count or a page count or a specific section from your outline, give yourself something that can be objectively measured. It doesn't matter if your goal is to write a thousand words, to write a page, or to cross off two sections from the outline—what matters is that it's tangible and you can see progress happening every time you sit down to work on your book, because progress tends to beget more progress. This milestone mapping makes writing the draft into a far more manageable task, because you're not trying to do the entire thing all at once.

Again, this is analogous to exercise—you wouldn't try to run a marathon tomorrow if you haven't run a single day in the last ten years. If you've not been training for a long time previously, you would start with short runs, sprints, cross-training and that kind of thing. Don't try to write your draft in marathon form either—give yourself small milestones you can gradually build on that will eventually get you across the finish line.

Once you're immersed in writing whatever the specific piece is for the day, allow yourself to follow your train of thought. Yes, you have a structure built—which is hopefully very detailed— but often you'll have an unexpected idea or you'll find an interesting way of exploring a particular topic that's a little different to what you had originally planned. And if that happens, roll with it. Remember that the outline is a living organism, and is going to change throughout the project, so if you've come up with a surprising or interesting way to present the information, then embrace that. While writing business books is not an artistic endeavor, necessarily, it *is* a creative endeavor. There's a lot of opportunity for you to explore your creativity as you communicate the concepts that form your book. The ideas that come to you when you're writing are probably going to be a bit different to the ones that you had when you were building the outline, because it's a different way of thinking. Building the outline is a technical and linear stage, whereas this is a much more creative stage, more intuitive and spontaneous.

Obviously, you want to keep to the main ideas you need to communicate, but let yourself have some fun with it. This part is where you get to make some magic and explore the way your mind works. Don't edit yourself too much, and trust your knowledge. You're obviously an expert in your field—if you are confident enough in your domain expertise to have committed to writing a book, then trust where your mind goes.

I also suggest working sequentially through your outline. This is partly because it appeals to my sense of orderliness, but it also is the best way to ensure that nothing gets missed. If you are jumping back and forth between different chapters, you can end up with a big old mess. Maybe you feel like writing a particular chapter one day, but then the next day you're a bit out of sorts and you don't feel like going back and filling in the gap, and then that missing piece doesn't get filled in until it's crunch time and you have to finish the draft. That can really break up the flow of the material for the reader—the continuity of your voice and the rhythm of each particular section is going to be a little bit different if you chop and change the sections you're working on. Aim for continuity wherever possible.

If you have ideas about a section that you're not working on at the moment, then by all means, make notes. You don't have to lose out on ideas or ignore moments of inspiration just because you're working in a different section. But just make a note of it— don't interrupt yourself and get out of order. One of the best books ever written on this topic—*On Writing Well*, by William

Zinsser—sums this up: "Clear thinking becomes clear writing. One can't exist without the other."

When your thinking is all over the place, jumping back and forth between different topics, then the writing is most likely going to reflect that confusion. Keep it as linear and structured and sequential as possible, while allowing for those creative moments to jump out at you.

SETTLING ON STYLE

Another thing that trips people up is the question of style. I think that style is largely a question of taste, and that instead of trying to write just like someone else has done, you should write as you feel comfortable. Don't try to wedge yourself into writing in a very formal way if your natural style is chatty and casual. If you have a sophisticated style, then don't dumb it down. Be yourself! Communicating in writing is no different to communicating in person—everybody responds better when you are communicating in the way that is comfortable for you.

Not only that, but the people who are going to do business with you will get a consistent experience. Remember the concept of creating congruence across the experiences they have with your business? If you have a very academic or thorough way of speaking, they'll be expecting that in how you write. If you have a very informal way of speaking, if you're very colloquial and chatty, then they will feel comfortable with seeing you write that way. Whatever your style, just be consistent. Once you're on a roll with a particular style, keep it up. Don't switch back and forth from formal to informal, or from complex academic language to chatty slang or banter.

Ultimately, aiming for simplicity and clarity in your style will keep you pretty safe. Always try to be as specific as possible— sweeping generalizations, cliches or vague implications just alienate readers. Use the simplest vocabulary possible to explain each concept, and say it in as few words as possible (using more words might make you feel smart, but it's not going to help the reader understand what you're talking about any more effectively).

WHAT TO DO ABOUT WRITER'S BLOCK

First, let me say that I believe that having writer's block is *not* an inevitability for authors. As far as I can tell, it happens most often when there's not enough clarity in your plan for producing the book, or when you're not taking care of yourself.

If you are looking at a blank page, with the cursor blinking at you and you just feel completely stuck, then go back to your outline and look at whether your notes are detailed enough for the section you are supposed to be working on that day. If the section in your outline just has a vague overview statement, or is a 'note to self' with very little detail added to it, then maybe you need to go back and flesh that out. Break the overarching idea down into its constituent parts, and put down as much detail as you can manage in bullet points beneath the heading. Make a note of all the relevant theoretical information a reader would need, all your examples and stories and experiences, and any research that you will need to do, so that when you go back to the page to start writing, you're ready to start tying all of that together.

Sometimes if you feel stuck, it's that you are too close to the material. You're getting too deep in the weeds or you're going around in circles and you can't get enough of a birds-eye view of the material to write about it effectively. And if that's the case, take a break. Step away from the writing, and do something else that's fun and creative. Maybe it's playing with your kids or your dog, going on a little adventure in your town or meeting up with someone you love hanging out with for a spontaneous catch-up. Play is a critical part of creativity and creation—psychiatrist and author Dr. Stuart Brown, MD, found in his research that play at work can increase creativity, productivity, engagement and morale. He says, "Play is games, art, books, sports, movies, music, comedy, flirting, talking and even daydreaming."[3]

When you step away to play for an hour or two, you give your brain a moment to come up with a solution. A lot of the time, a really knotty problem in writing will resolve itself with just a little bit of time being left alone in your mind. Give yourself that space to allow your creativity to come up to the surface as it's needed.

If you're really tied up in knots, you can always ask someone who knows what you're doing to help you out with it. Grab your phone, hit record on your voice app and just hash it out with them. Tell them what you're stuck with and have them ask you questions about it to see what comes out of that conversation. Often you'll find some really interesting material—the conversation will jog your mind, give you some new perspective and get you energized again. Many people—especially entrepreneurs and business leaders, who are used to explaining complex concepts verbally—do really well in an interview format. This is exactly the process that I use with all of my ghostwriting and coaching clients, because once you've got the outline, the easiest way to get a lot of great material produced is to talk it through together. You can use your outline as the basis for interview questions, or each section as a way to start a new conversation. (Note that this material then provides the basis for the material you will write afterwards—as I mentioned earlier, an unedited transcription should not be used as final material.)

If your writer's block is not a structural problem, then maybe there's an environmental problem. Sometimes if you're in a space where there are lots of people, it can be very distracting and hard to get in the zone. On the other hand, if you're in an environment where it's extremely quiet and completely still, the silence can weigh on you and start to feel oppressive and distracting in itself—maybe going somewhere with a little bit more energy and vibrance would help you get that creativity going again. Sometimes the solution is just getting into a new location to write.

Other times, it's your internal environment that's disrupted. We all get into situations where we're tired or stressed or hungover or hungry or grumpy. Sitting down to write is often the first moment we've actually had enough peace to realize that something is wrong, and it can be almost impossible to get your head in the game if something is messing with you. If that's the situation you find yourself in, then take a walk, do a workout, go sit in the sun and meditate, or take a nap. I have decided on many, many days that it would be far more productive to take the afternoon off to get myself sorted out, rather than trying to grind through writing. I know it's at odds with knocking off your daily milestone, but the stuff that you write when you are really distracted or irritated or whatever is probably not going to be great material anyway. It's better to rearrange your schedule a little bit so you can do whatever you need to in order to feel energized and focused, so you can come back to the writing feeling fresh.

Sometimes you will just really need a break. If you're stressed out, not sleeping well, or you have a lot going on in another part of your life, you might physically feel your well of creativity draining. On a random Thursday morning, you might sit down, open your computer and realize, *I am empty. I have nothing to say right now.* Even though you might have total clarity about what you need to write next, and who you're writing for, you have absolutely no way to get it out of you and onto the page.

And if that's the case, it is okay.

The project will still be there in a couple of days (or weeks, or however long it takes). It's far better to take a pause to look after yourself, than to grind yourself down to a pulp trying to stick to an arbitrary schedule. Deal with whatever needs your attention, do whatever you need to in order to take care of yourself and get back to equilibrium. The material you produce as a result will be *much* better, and the process will also be sustainable. You can't write if you're dead, or your life is burning down all around you. Addiction, relationship breakdown and health catastrophes abound in the history of writing, and there is absolutely no reason for you to join that tradition. Your book should be a positive addition to your life, not the straw that breaks the camel's back. If you find yourself struggling under the load, give yourself permission to prioritize appropriately in order to make this project a sustainable part of the rest of your life.

5

EDITING

ONCE YOU'VE FINISHED YOUR DRAFT, YOU'RE GOING TO HEAVE a huge sigh of relief. It's a massive achievement to have put into words everything you know about your field, and you should take some time to celebrate.

That said, the draft is only half the process. Editing is how the book really becomes what the reader will engage with, and it's a critical part of the process. I would argue that without a thorough editing process of a professional standard, your book should not be published—partly because it's going to be full of typos and errors, and partly because you may not have honed your message sufficiently to really communicate what you mean to your readers.

Editing is about taking the raw, rough material of the draft and paring it down to say exactly what you mean in the most compelling way possible. The point of writing this book is to clearly communicate something that's important for your audience, and if you send it out in that rough draft format, they're probably going to miss the key points that they wanted to learn in the first place. There might be discrepancies in the information, there's going to be emphasis on the wrong things— where unimportant or tangential ideas or information get more focus than necessary—and pieces will be out of order or incomplete.

Please understand that I am not summarily passing judgement on your skills here—every single author, no matter how seasoned, is in the same boat when they finish their first draft, myself included. And every published author understands that editing is an essential part of ensuring that the reader gets the book that they expected.

Now, editing is not a simple process. Unfortunately, it often takes as much time as writing the draft itself (or more), so you need to set aside a significant amount of time and energy to manage this part of the process. Allow yourself more time than you think you will need for editing. It's hard to give a prescriptive amount of time for this part of the process—it depends on how long your book is and how experienced you are —but I would say that if you are working on your own and it took you three months to write the draft, you should give yourself another three months to edit.

(Note that six months is a *very* respectable timeline to produce a book if you are working on it by yourself. Working with a professional writer can halve that time, but most self-directed authors will take a year or more to finish and publish their book.)

RESTING THE MANUSCRIPT

The first thing to do once you've finished your draft is to rest the manuscript. Put it in a drawer or close the file on your computer, and don't look at it for a while. Try to give yourself at least a few days or a week. Stephen King famously puts his manuscripts away for six weeks before he starts editing, and the reason for this is that you need to get a bit of distance from it. You've been so immersed in producing the draft material that your brain is crammed with ideas and information, and you will lack the perspective to see what's missing or will need correction.

Ultimately, you want to come back to the manuscript with fresh eyes, feeling energized and ready to throw yourself in again. By this point you probably will have forgotten about a lot of the material you wrote, or at least won't feel like it's too familiar.

THE STRUCTURAL FIRST PASS

Once you've rested the manuscript, it's time for a structural first pass. This is where you read through the manuscript on your computer (assuming you typed it, rather than handwrote it) and correct any obvious problems.

This first pass is about looking for flaws in the flow of the material. When you notice something that feels out of place, move it around into a section where it fits more naturally. The information should flow in a logical sequence that makes it easy for the reader to follow you from one thought to the next. If you're jumping back and forth across multiple ideas or points, then it's key to smooth that out in order to create a cohesive experience for the reader.

If you've been working to a clear and detailed outline, then hopefully that cohesion will have been established organically during the drafting process. But it's very common, even for experienced writers, to find that something is a bit out place. Often the solution is as simple as swapping a paragraph with the one before—the information itself is all good, but you just need to present it in a slightly different arrangement so that it is as logical and easy for the reader to absorb as possible.

You're also looking for obvious spelling mistakes, grammatical errors, missing words, and giant walls of text that can be broken up into smaller paragraphs. Occasionally you'll notice inconsistencies throughout your text ('OK' versus 'okay', quotes formatted differently and so on) and you can make notes to yourself as you go along to check the entire text for these during the copy edit later on.

This structural first pass is often quite a long process. You'll be reading through the whole draft, and it's best to do this one chapter at a time. Edit your chapters in sequence, reading through one chapter, making sure that everything is smooth, then moving onto the next chapter, checking that each chapter flows naturally into the next. Remember that the point here is not to fix every tiny little thing—this round of editing is about the flow of information and fixing any glaring errors (including fact-checking).

Sometimes you'll find that pieces need to be moved into other chapters, and when that's the case then you may need to rework those sections a bit to make sure that the new structure flows well. Occasionally, you'll realize that a whole chapter needs to be reworked or removed or placed in a different position in the book. If a chapter is really not working—if it's really vague, not useful or confusing—then it's worth the effort of reworking it. If a reader is jarred out of the flow of what they're reading, there's a good chance they'll just put the book down and never come back to it. Your goal is to make sure that they stay as engaged and compelled to keep reading as possible. If you're resisting changing something significant, ask if *you* would persevere with this section—if you wouldn't, there's no chance in hell that a reader will.

EARLY READERS

Once you've done your structural edit, you've made sure that everything is flowing neatly, and that all of the obvious errors have been corrected, then it's time to give the manuscript to your early readers. Select two or three people who understand your industry and/or your business, and who will be ready and willing to give you honest feedback on the book.

Good candidates are business partners, mentors, mastermind partners or qualified friends. Don't give it to your mother or your significant other looking for praise or a pat on the head; that can come later, when you *know* you've done the best job possible and deserve the adulation. No, this is where you volunteer your work for a gauntlet of criticism, challenge and questioning.

If your early readers are worth their salt, you're going to have a lot of feedback. But to make your book stand the test of time —and the attention of thousands of curious, intelligent, critical readers—you have to get in the arena with them.

Explain to your early readers that you need their help to make the material as robust as possible. Have them make notes throughout the manuscript where they are confused, where information is missing, where they get bored, where they want more explanation, where there could be examples or stories. This is why you need early readers who are *qualified* to comment on the type of material that you're communicating. Their criticism needs to be constructive and relevant—not useless complaints about whether you double space after periods, or lecturing you about why you should really use the Oxford comma.

This is a very important stage, because if you have been doing this by yourself, it's easy to end up in an echo chamber. You can start to believe that everything you've produced is perfect, when in reality, it only makes sense to you, and no one else. Or you can be gripped by a constant and debilitating belief that everything you've written is absolute rubbish and you should just throw it all away and forget the whole idea. The role of your early readers is to save you from yourself, regardless of which camp you find yourself in. Yes, it's scary to let other people read your draft and invite their comments. Yes, those comments can be painful and frustrating and make you want to throw your computer out the window. This quote from Teddy Roosevelt can be helpful to keep in mind at this stage (and even if it seems hyperbolic to you right now, it won't in the moment):

> It is not the critic who counts; not the man who points out how
> the strong man stumbles, or where the doer of deeds could have

done them better. The credit belongs to the man who is actually in the arena, whose face is marred by dust and sweat and blood; who strives valiantly; who errs, who comes short again and again, because there is no effort without error and shortcoming; but who does actually strive to do the deeds; who knows great enthusiasms, the great devotions; who spends himself in a worthy cause; who at the best knows in the end the triumph of high achievement, and who at the worst, if he fails, at least fails while daring greatly, so that his place shall never be with those cold and timid souls who neither know victory nor defeat.[1]

Take heart that you have produced something valuable and that you have people in your life who care enough about your success to help you protect that work from undue criticism or avoidable failures. This gauntlet of feedback is the first step into the arena, so if you feel you have come up short, or erred in too many places, throw yourself back in, and keep at it until you reach that point of triumph.

IN ORDER TO MANAGE YOUR EARLY READERS, I RECOMMEND creating a copy of the original document for them to share. It's very easy to do this in Google Docs, and you can just give them the ability to comment—*not* to edit. (The last thing you want is for three or four people to be editing the original material, because you won't be able to keep track of what has been changed. They should just be able to highlight the section they are referring to and make a comment on the text, so that you can track everything that is being discussed without losing the original material.)

Sometimes you're going to get feedback from an early reader that you disagree with. Stephen King says in the foreword to his memoir, *On Writing*, that "no writer will take all of his or her editor's advice; for all have sinned and fallen short of editorial perfection. Put another way, to write is human, to edit is divine."[2] If you choose to ignore the (potentially divine) suggestions of your early readers or editors, make sure you can rationally defend your decision. Now, if everybody says that a particular part doesn't make sense to them, or that something needs to be reworked, then I would take that collective wisdom and pay attention to it, even if it's not your view. If all your early readers react the same way, you can expect your general readers to react that way too. If you really disagree with them, then have a conversation about whether the material itself is problematic or if the issue would be resolved with a rewrite to make it more palatable or accessible. Use your judgment— ultimately you are going to know the material in the most depth, but where there's smoke there's fire, and so if you're getting a lot of feedback about particular parts, try to work it in.

Once you've had the early readers go through the complete manuscript, you will need to spend some time implementing all of their changes and working on all of their suggestions, then smoothing out anything that has gotten messy in that process. If there have been major additions or changes to the structure as a result of the early reader feedback, then it's time to go back and repeat the structural first pass—make sure that all the new material is in the right position, that it all flows smoothly, and that there are no obvious errors. Once you've done that, rest the manuscript again for a few more days.

COPY EDITING

Once you have gone through and implemented all of the early reader commentary, it's time for a copy edit. This is where you start looking for the technical errors in the work—at this stage all the big elements are in place, and we're onto looking for cosmetic issues. This includes correct spelling and grammar, correct use of language, and consistency across all of the information.

This round of editing should happen on paper—not on your screen. Print your manuscript and read it out loud to yourself with a bright pen in hand, going line by line, to make sure that every word and symbol is correct. If most of your pages end up looking like a toddler got hold of them with a magic marker, don't worry. The eye spots errors on paper that it skips right over on a screen, and reading it out loud will highlight any errors in syntax or flow.

If you are not confident in your grasp on spelling, grammar and syntax, I highly recommend hiring a professional editor at this stage. There are so many quirks in language that can trip you up here, and while it's completely understandable to make mistakes, readers can be brutal in their criticisms of poor copy editing. This part of the editing process might seem like it's just polishing the surface, but that surface will dictate, almost exclusively, the reader's instinctive reactions to the work.

If you do choose to do the copy editing yourself, here are key things to look out for:

- Crutch words: these are words that you use reflexively, over and over again. These tend to be words like 'really', 'just', 'so'—filler words that help you emphasize something or connect two ideas together. Or maybe you default to describing good things as 'incredible', 'amazing', or 'awesome', instead of varying your descriptions. Everyone has their own unique crutch words, and you'll most likely come across yours when reading the manuscript out loud—hearing a word over and over will highlight it to you.
- Always use the simplest, clearest language you can. This is not about dumbing down your message; it's about communicating as effectively as possible. Don't make your reader work hard to understand you, or

you will lose them. For example, it's much easier to understand "he hid his plans and kept changing his mind" than "his intent was obfuscated and he prevaricated interminably." Keep your language simple and clear.

- Check that terminology and jargon is being used consistently. For example, if you've used a term in one context in an early chapter, and then use it differently later on, that's going to confuse the reader. Ensure that any abbreviations or acronyms are explained the first time they are introduced, to orient any readers who are unfamiliar with them.
- Make sure any facts or statements are verified and that you have added add footnotes or references to give evidence of your claims.
- Remove redundancies and unnecessary repetitions. (Sometimes you'll repeat yourself to make a point, and that's fine, but it's important to acknowledge it when you do that.) Redundant words add unnecessary detail to a phrase. For example, in the phrase, "She wandered slowly through the park," 'slowly' is redundant, because the pace of her movement is implied in the word 'wandering.'
- Always choose the most accurate word to communicate your meaning. For example, "She ran quickly through the field" would be more effective as "she sprinted through the field."
- Be careful with adjectives and adverbs. Adjectives are 'describing' words: 'bright,' 'crisp,' 'lazy.' Verbs ('doing' words: 'run,' 'fizz,' 'think') are modified by adverbs, which describe *how* a verb is happening: 'brightly,' 'crisply,' 'lazily'. Adjectives and adverbs can add color to your writing, but they can make it very dense when used too often.
- Avoid unnecessary mannerisms. For example, an

excessive use of ellipses (those three dots that can indicate... a pause), writing in capital letters, ending phrases with exclamation points, or breaking down paragraphs into single lines. This kind of thing can become very tiresome for the reader, so again, select the most accurate phrasing to make your point as clearly as possible, rather than relying on fancy formatting.

- Finally, if you're unsure about the spelling of a word, or the correct grammar in a phrase, just Google it. Someone else has almost certainly already looked it up (and created some content about it), and there's no shame in checking.

All your written edits should then be added to your working document. Many writers will do two or more rounds of copy editing, simply because they found so many errors in the first round that they want to make sure they got them all. This is also a good opportunity to sign off on the material—there will be a final round of proofreading once the book has been formatted and is ready for publication, just to ensure that the conversion from working document to print document didn't create any problems, but your manuscript should be publication-ready by the end of your copy editing.

EDITING IS A LONG PROCESS, AND IT'S INCREDIBLY IMPORTANT, so there's an endless amount of argument about when you should stop. There comes a point where you start getting diminishing returns on your editing, and I would say that if you haven't noticed something to be fixed after four rounds, you're probably not going to notice it. At some point you have to put your trust in the publishing gods and release it.

Don't worry; if there are errors, your readers will let you

know, and the great thing with self-publishing is that you can correct those errors down the line if you want to. Rest assured that even traditional publishers—who do this exclusively as their business—still occasionally have errors make it into the final product. As long as you have been thorough and diligent in your editing (seriously, hire an editor) there should be very few errors, and the most important thing is that your message is clearly, succinctly communicated, that readers get the information they want and need, and that they are compelled to act as you have hoped they will.

TITLE AND COVER DESIGN

TITLING YOUR BOOK IS ONE OF THE MOST IMPORTANT CHOICES that you'll make in this entire project. Unfortunately, it's also a decision that many writers leave to the very end of the process, when they are about to be crushed by their deadline and don't have the necessary time to make a good decision. And plenty of writers give it almost no thought at all, as if it were some throwaway task that has to get done for the book to be published.

In reality, this is one of the most influential marketing decisions that you'll make for the book, and it will often have a very significant impact on how the book performs. It will affect your sales volume, it will affect whether word of mouth will take off, and it will even have an impact on whether readers take the action you are trying to lead them to.

This is equally true for the cover design (also known as jacket design or artwork). People do judge books by their covers—this is literally why that saying exists. How often have you been in a bookshop and picked up a book specifically because the title appealed to you, or the cover design really stood out? These two factors are probably the most influential among all of the customer buying decisions, and I beg you not to treat them as an afterthought.

Most customers are influenced by a whole host of factors, and often these are completely unconscious, but among them are:

- The title of the book
- The recommending source (where they first heard about the book)
- The book cover
- The description on the back or on the sales page,
- The blurbs and reviews
- The author bio and picture
- The length of the book
- The text itself when they look inside
- The price

The title is the most important of all of those features because it tells people what they will get. Responding to the title makes them identify themselves as being part of your audience—like a psychological opt-in box. This creates a need for consistency (where their actions align with their perception of themselves), and need for consistency leads to purchasing behavior (*'That's a catchy title. Oh yeah—Famous Guy likes this book! Cool cover. All the info on the cover sounds like stuff I need to know... guess I'd better get it'*).

CHOOSING A TITLE

Before we jump in, let me say a little something to the folks who have decided on the title of their book before they've ever written a word: that can work, if you've truly got something great, but it can also trip you up. When you get very attached to a title early in the piece, it becomes difficult to change your mind later on, even if it becomes apparent that everyone else hates it or they don't get it. Try to keep an open mind, even if you think you've got something unbeatable. Go through this process and test your title to make sure that your readers think it is as good as you do.

～

THERE ARE MANY DIFFERENT WAYS THAT YOU CAN GO ABOUT creating the title for your book, but there are some general rules of thumb for you to keep in mind when you are doing all of your brainstorming.

The first thing you want to focus on is making sure that it grabs attention. This is the title's main job, and it absolutely must perform. The title does a ton of heavy lifting just to get a reader to pick up the book in the first place, because it is competing with so many other books trying to do the same thing. Remember that your readers are exposed to so much content every day that your title really has to stop them in their tracks.

You can do that by leading with a promise, like you saw with *The 4-Hour Workweek, The Ten Day MBA* and *The $100 Start-Up*. Provocative titles can often work, like *Winners Take All, Hooked,* and *Ignore Everybody*. Something a bit strange, like *Shoe Dog, Purple Cow* or *The Hard Thing About Hard Things* can make people take note, particularly when you have a strong personal brand behind the book. Another option is to make up a word, or to use a powerful single word: *Outliers, Essentialism, Influence*. Or again, you can rely on being clear and simple to catch someone's attention: *The One Thing, 80/20 Sales and Marketing, Permission Marketing*.

Your title does not have to be controversial or clever. Those approaches do work, but the main point here is to get someone's attention long enough that they think, *'That sounds like something I want to know.'*

The next thing that you need to factor in is making the title easy to remember. Sometimes people will hear about a book on a podcast, or they'll see a link to it in an article, or someone will tell them about it in a conversation. If the title is not memorable, they might vaguely remember the topic, or the reason it seemed relevant to them, but if they can't remember the title there's little chance they will ever find it. Let's say your book is about business operations. They can't remember your name, or the name of the book, and start Googling 'book about business operations'. You can imagine how that's going to go. While your marketing might make it show up, or maybe the name will come back to them, you want to give yourself the best possible advantage here by making sure there's some memorable element to the title.

Part of making a memorable title is making it informative. If the potential reader would have to ask you what the book was about after hearing the title, then it's probably not informative enough. They should get a sense of the book's big idea from the title, so that they cross a decision threshold where they identify that it's interesting and relevant to them. This is particularly important in business books, where the reader has high expectations of quality information, and where you are competing with all the other demands on their time.

However, your title does not have to do all the heavy lifting alone. Subtitles are extremely common, and you can use one to expand or explain the main title. For example, *Linchpin: Are You Indispensable?*, *Originals: How Non-Conformists Move the World*, and *Influence: The Psychology of Persuasion* are all examples where the subtitle has added significant information for the reader to consider.

Another great example is *The End of Jobs: Money, Meaning and Freedom Without the 9-to-5*. Anybody looking for a new career, coming to the end of their college degree, or wondering about the future of work as AI and automation expand, will pick up this book. Between the title and the subtitle, you get an immediate sense of what the book is about and what you're going to get out of it. It's clear, it's informative, and it's memorable.

You can also use the subtitle to add in any keywords that you know people are looking for related to your business. A little SEO research here can go a long way here to help you identify what people are searching for, what other titles are performing well in your space, and how you can fill any holes in the market with your own title. If you can use the name of your book to create a clear differentiation from all the other material in the space, then you can build quite an advantage for yourself. It doesn't matter if the subtitle seems long—you just need to make sure that the main title is succinct, clear and interesting.

Another thing to factor in is whether your chosen title is going to pass the Bar Test. Not the legal one—imagine going into a bar on a busy Saturday night and shouting the title to your friend while you're standing in line to buy a drink. Can they understand you? Do you feel embarrassed shouting it in a crowded place? Would they feel comfortable if they were the one doing the shouting? If the title is awkward or embarrassing for people to say, you're going to have trouble getting your marketing off the ground.

It should also be physically easy to say. The longer and more wordy it is, the more difficult it will be to say, and the harder it will be for your reader to experience cognitive fluency with it. Cognitive fluency means that they can immediately say the title to themselves and understand exactly what it means. Keeping the title simple will allow them to maximize that cognitive fluency and to make a quick, often unconscious, decision about whether or not the book is right for them. Phrases from within the book, or important words from within the book, are often really great options here. If you're talking about a specific concept that you have coined, or something that is a critical driver in your business, then you should definitely add that to your list of potential titles.

Once you've got a few viable options, I recommend testing

your title ideas with your audience. Before you start, though, make sure that the web domains are available for each of the titles. It's very frustrating to finally come to a decision about your title, only to find that someone else already owns the domain, or worse, has an established brand of the same name. Once that's all squared away, the easiest way to test your titles is to go into your Facebook group or email list (or however you communicate with your audience) and share a quick survey or poll, asking them to vote on their favorite one. You can ask them to leave comments or feedback on why they like a particular title, or you can invite them to submit their own ideas. This is a great way of marketing to a warm audience, and getting buy-in from people who already know you—ensuring that they start to develop a small sense of ownership in the project and become invested in its success.

COVER DESIGN

Cover design is equally important in getting your book in front of the right readers as the title. The cover can communicate the intent of the book, what the reader is likely to experience, and it can either align your book with a niche, or it can set it apart.

Imagine going into a bookstore or browsing through Amazon without book covers to look at. It would be *so* difficult to ever make a purchasing decision, because if you were relying on titles alone, you would have to absorb far too much information to make an efficient decision. The cover, then, should be a visual representation of the content, almost like a mental shortcut to understanding what the book is about, so it's really important that the cover is both congruent with that material, and visually arresting.

Again, this is something that's often treated as an afterthought, which is why you've seen so many boring book covers—and forgotten them the moment you looked away. Often a particular genre of book will get into a trend with covers, and every book that comes out on that topic looks exactly the same. How many self-help books have someone looking wistfully out over a body of water? How many business books have a collection of vector images squished together? How many biographies have an extreme close-up of the subject's face? Normally a trend like this spins up because someone does something innovative, and then everyone else piles on, eventually turning that fresh new approach into a boring trope.

Having another same-same cover is the kiss of death for a book. If the cover is boring, people will assume the material is boring and they won't buy it. Readers are going to instinctively respond to that visual representation—the purpose of the book cover is to *show* the reader what they're going to get rather than *tell* them, so you have think about it as part of your marketing plan.

The cover is going to have just as much impact on whether somebody will pick it up in a bookstore as the title will. Are they going to be embarrassed to be seen holding that image in their hands, or will it make them feel like a bad-ass? Is it going to make them feel like they're part of the cool kids club, or like they're broken and a loser? Think about how the reader is going to identify themselves when they pick up that book.

HOW TO GET A GREAT COVER

And now for the most important piece of advice for this whole section: Do not design the cover yourself.

Unless you are a professional artist or designer, you have no business whatsoever designing that cover. You can see amateur cover design a mile away, and it's extremely damaging to the credibility of the book. If the cover is a hot mess, again, people will assume the content is too. Whipping up a cover for your book in Canva or Photoshop in an afternoon will not meet the quality standards that make a book stand out on a shelf and make readers take it seriously.

Getting a great cover—that is a clear visual representation of the material—is about writing a good design brief. A lot of people stumble here, because they try to explain an idea or a feeling without specifics. "I'll know when I see it," is not a design brief, nor is it useful feedback to give a designer, so before you submit any kind of design brief to your book cover designer, do your research. Build up a portfolio of images and inspiration that give the designer a sense of what you like and what kind of design elements need to be included. They will need to know the title, subtitle, author attributions and any additional textual material you want to include on the front cover, as well as having at least a draft for the back cover material (blurb, endorsements, and bio) so they can generate the first round of designs.

Once you've got a rough idea of the design elements that you like and the kind of covers that you want to use as inspiration, then it's time to find your designer. Working with 99designs (www.99designs.com) is a great option for most people, or if you want to work with someone specific, then reach out to them with your brief. (If there are book covers you really love, you can usually find the cover design credit on the inside of that book, and then you can just Google that artist or designer to get in touch with them.) Either way, give your designer as much detail and as many examples as possible—within a theme. Don't give them five examples that are completely different; give them five examples that are thematically consistent, and will give them a good foundation to work from.

Once you've got a shortlist of designs, go back to your audience and poll them. Often, the people that helped with the title are going to be useful to helping with the cover too—they have already given a lot of thought to your project and have a clear sense of what you're trying to achieve with the book.

Choose a cover that elicits a strong reaction from people, something that people either love or hate. Hopefully there'll be a lot of love, but if plenty of people love it and a handful hate it, that's often really a good sign. Either way, it is grabbing people's attention, and it will generate interest simply by the strong reaction it provokes.

Remember, too, that you are not your audience. What appeals to them may not appeal to you, and while there are occasionally circumstances to override popular opinion, for the most part, I would advise paying attention to the options that elicit the strongest reactions from your audience and choosing one of them.

Once you've settled on your design, finesse any final details with your designer. Don't forget that the cover design for the physical format is not just the front of the book, but also the spine and back cover. In order for the spine width to be accurate, you will need to provide a final page count and trim size to the designer, along with an ISBN and barcode (which will be covered in the next chapter on typesetting and publication). You will need to write a back cover blurb describing what the book is about, collect any testimonials you want to include, and write your author bio, provide your headshot, and make sure it will all fit with the trim size you have chosen.

Note that cover design can take anywhere from two weeks to well over a month, so be sure that you start work on your cover at least a few weeks before you want to list the book for publication.

❧ 7 ❧

TYPESETTING AND PUBLICATION

T YPESETTING (ALSO CALLED INTERIOR DESIGN) IS THE PROCESS of formatting and designing the layout of the book to be print-ready. Again, this is an area where I *strongly* recommend working with a professional interior designer or formatter. While it seems like formatting should be a relatively simple task, it's actually quite complex and requires a stunning amount of attention to detail.

There are dozens of little decisions that need to be made, which may seem unimportant, but can have a significant impact on how the reader interacts with the book. Typesetting goes almost completely unnoticed, except when it goes wrong. For example, some typefaces and line justifications will give readers headaches. Particular paragraph alignments can completely break a reader's focus, and margin width can determine whether the text is overextended into the binding area, therefore becoming difficult to read.

K EY DECISIONS ABOUT TYPSETTING INCLUDE:

- Trim size (the physical size of the book)

- Paper stock and color
- Paperback versus hardback
- Binding style
- Typography
- Page margins and gutters
- Spacing decisions
- Design elements
- Sidebars
- Graphics

Typesetting is also the last chance to have someone else proofread the manuscript, and many designers will have an eye for the tiny details that can get missed in copyediting—incorrect uses of hyphens and em/en dashes, differences in quotation marks, symbols and other punctuation, as well as accidental spacings and so on.

Not only is all this very involved, but the process is also different for print books and ebooks. Of course, that's no reason to shy away from producing both formats—while it is a little easier to do the design and formatting for an ebook, ebooks don't have quite the same impact a physical book does. Many people choose not to publish a physical format, and while it's understandable, it is a small signal that can undercut the credibility and positioning of your project. Not only does publishing a physical format subtly increase the authority associated with the book, it's an easy way to set yourself apart from a potentially crowded ebook market, and to open up significantly more opportunities to put the book to work. You can't give away ebooks at events or speaking engagements, you can't send personalized copies to clients and prospects, and you can't really throw a launch party or book event without physical copies for people to pick up and physically engage with.

As I said, I strongly recommend working with a designer to get all the various elements of your interior design right. However, book interior designers are in extremely high demand because the process is so involved. A viable alternative, if you have limited time or budget, is a piece of software called Vellum (www.vellum.pub). It's a basic solution that will limit the variables you can apply to each format, but it will allow you to customize the interior design of both ebook and physical formats, and ensure that each is correctly formatted for submission to the various publishing platforms. At the time of writing, Vellum is only available for use on the Mac-OS and costs $249.99 for unlimited physical and ebook creations. They have a thorough tutorial program, and while the actual conversion of the documents will only take a few minutes, you will need to spend a couple of hours playing around with each of the different elements to ensure that everything comes out right. You will need to create MOBI files for listing the ebook on Kindle, EPUB files for listing the ebook elsewhere (this is the universal standard; Amazon just likes having their own format), and a PDF file for listing the physical version for your print-on-demand service.

Below are a few key things you need to think about when formatting your book for publication.

TRIM SIZE

The trim is the size of the physical format of the book. Trims are measured in inches, with the horizontal measurement followed by the vertical measurement. The industry standard size for all formats is 6 × 9, though it's common to use 5.5 × 8.5 for business books (the physical format of this book is 5.5 × 8.5). You can choose trim sizes smaller than that, but they start to look and feel somewhat awkward for the reader, while larger trims can start to look like textbooks.

PAGE MARGINS AND GUTTERS

The page margins are the negative space around the text on

the page. The gutters (also known as the inside margins) are the adjacent inner margins of the two pages when the book is open —the space that goes down to where each page is joined to the binding. Proper margins provide critical visual balance to the page, making it far easier for the eye to pass over all the text. The standard size for margins is half an inch, while the gutter is usually 25 to 50% wider to prevent the text from sliding down into the binding. The title and author name are traditionally included in the top margins, while page numbers are usually included in the bottom margins.

TYPOGRAPHY

Typography, or font selection, is a surprisingly important choice for your book. The type used can have a profound impact on how the reader engages with the book—some fonts are very easy and calming to read, while others can be distracting and difficult. Some fonts look very professional, while others look completely amateur.

Look for options that are clearly legible in all forms—italic, bold and caps should all be equally easy to read. Your font of choice should also include title and header formats that are neat and legible (for use at the beginning of new sections).

There are both serif and sans serif fonts that fit this bill (serif fonts have little flourishes at the edges of each letter; sans serif fonts do not—for example, Times New Roman is a serif font, while Arial is sans serif). Serif fonts tend to look traditional and conservative, while sans serif fonts look a little more clean and modern.

FRONT MATTER

Front matter is the material that you include at the very beginning of the book—details about the publishing imprint, the copyright claim, printing editions and location of those printings, along with the ISBN, author notes, design credit and various other details about publication. If you register the work for copyright, you can also include the Library of Congress data here. You can look at the first couple of pages in any book to find the front matter—usually it's on the left-hand page, opposite the dedication or title page. You can also consider a collection of endorsements as part of the front matter—if you are going to include a selection of rave reviews, put them before the other front matter, as the very first material the reader will see when they open the book.

HOW TO LIST YOUR BOOK FOR PUBLICATION

Once you have created your files, make sure you spend some time proofreading them. This is that final round I mentioned in the chapter on editing—it's crucial to check that no errors have been generated in the conversion process. Common errors include line breaks in incorrect locations, additional spaces between paragraphs, and blank pages inserted where they should not be. Check that quotes have been indented, bullet lists are correct, all quotation marks are correct, and that there are no missing words throughout the text. When you are satisfied that the files are perfect, confirm the final page count with your cover designer so they can guarantee that the width of the spine design will be accurate, and then you can get into the actual process of publication.

Now, you can choose to publish exclusively through Amazon's Kindle Direct Publishing platform, and that's a very easy choice. Amazon's platforms account for 70% of all books purchased online It allows you to list your ebook version and physical version on Kindle together, though if you choose to produce an audio version, you will have to list it separately through Amazon's Audiobook Creation Exchange (ACX)—this is the audiobook platform that will feed your title through to

Audible. Currently this option is only available to authors with a US or UK tax ID.

The other major player in the self-publishing space is Ingram Spark. They have a much broader distribution network than KDP, and will list your book on more than 39,000 retailers and libraries all over the world, including all the major channels—Amazon, Barnes & Noble, Apple iBooks, Kobo, and more. Obviously, this is extremely beneficial in reaching additional audiences who are not purchasing all their books through Amazon (and you can still list your book on ACX, as it's an independent platform from the other Amazon properties).

KDP also has a separate platform called Author Central, where you can set up an author profile page that your book listing will link to. This is where you can list a more in-depth biography, post reviews and testimonials, and will become a central repository for all your works listed on KDP should you choose to publish multiple books. You can also link to blog posts on your own site, which is obviously good for your site's rankings and for your ability to capture additional traffic from Amazon, which you would not otherwise be able to do. Setting up your author profile is not strictly essential, but it develops trust and visibility on the platform, and most importantly, gives you the ability to add Editorial Reviews to the sales pages of your books (a huge opportunity for building the book's credibility and influencing buying decisions).

KDP says that when you sign up to Author Central, "it can take 3 to 5 days for the Author Page to appear on the Amazon.com site. You can begin adding content to an Author Page as soon as you sign up. Once your Author Central account is set up and approved by a publisher, changes appear on the Author Page within 24 hours of the time you add them in Author Central."

KDP, ACX and IngramSpark all have extensive documentation on how to list your book in all formats, which I won't reproduce here, because the platforms also include wizards that will direct you through the entire process. Before you start, though, it's worth ensuring that you have everything you need for this process ready to go, so here's a quick checklist:

- Formatted, designed, proofread manuscript.
- Completed cover for the ebook format and the physical format (which requires a complete wrap-around cover—front, spine with accurate width, and back).
- Author bio and profile picture.
- Blurb for the sales page, including any testimonials.
- Category and keywords you intend to list the book in (you can research this by simply visiting the Kindle website and clicking through all the relevant categories listed there and looking at how many books are listed in each, to get a feel for how much competition you will have in each one).
- ISBN (if you are providing your own).

You will be asked for various metadata to be included in publication, and this is where we need to have The Talk about ISBNs and barcodes and copyright. Please forgive me.

DEALING WITH ISBNS

An ISBN (International Standard Book Number) is a unique, internationally-recognized number that registers your book and all the data associated with it across all sales platforms. According to Bowker, who provides all ISBNs, "the 13 digit ISBN links to essential information used in sales tracking, retail inventory systems, library catalogs, bookstores, online stores, and for new digital editions for old books."[1]

Each format of your book needs a unique ISBN, so if you are publishing an ebook, physical book, and audiobook, you will need three ISBNs. If you are printing two formats of the physical book—a soft cover and a hard cover—each of those will need a unique ISBN as well.

ISBNs are sold by country, but are recognized internationally, so you only have to buy them once for each of your formats to be listed globally. Bowker and its subsidiaries are the central location for purchasing ISBNs, though some countries will provide ISBNs free of charge to self-publishing authors. You can buy an individual ISBN ($125), or you can buy a pack of 10 ($295). It makes far more sense to buy the 10-pack if you are publishing multiple formats, and just keeping your additional ISBNs for your next book.

Yes, this is a racket. And yes, you can get around it, but as always, there are consequences.

Many people balk at paying such high prices for a random string of numbers, and justifiably so. Amazon, seeing how frequently this barrier to entry was getting in the way of people publishing more, decided to offer ISBNs for free—in exchange for exclusive distribution of the work. So you save the money up front, but you don't control where you can sell your book (note that this means you can't sell it directly from a sales page on your own website—you have to send all would-be buyers to Amazon). For many authors outside the business genre, this is a non-issue—if you're writing teen fiction, for example, selling exclusively on Amazon makes total sense. But when the book is going to be a key part of the marketing infrastructure of your business, retaining that control over distribution is extremely important.

Another critical factor is controlling the metadata and publishing imprint associated with your work (the publishing imprint is who is credited with publishing the work, and in your case, it might be your name, or the name of your business. Traditional imprints you might be familiar with include Random House, Penguin, Simon & Schuster and so on). If you don't purchase your own ISBN, then KDP automatically becomes the publisher imprint. Not only that, but KDP will control the metadata about your book, including the book description listed on Kindle.

So while it is indeed a racket to buy your ISBNs through official channels, I think it's worth it in order to retain control of the distribution, rights and metadata of your work. You also need to buy barcodes for your physical formats. These are also sold in larger packages than most people need, and again, are sold by Bowker. Once you have purchased your ISBNs and barcodes, their set-up wizard will walk you through how to assign them to your book.

DEALING WITH COPYRIGHT

Copyright is another confusing aspect that you should understand before hitting Publish on your book. You will be asked if you own the copyright to the work, and the legal penalties for copyright infringement can be severe, so for anyone who is unfamiliar with this concept, copyright is 'the exclusive and assignable legal right, given to the originator for a fixed number of years, to print, publish, perform, film, or record literary, artistic, or musical material.'[2]

Copyright means that you own the material, and that no one else can reproduce it without your permission. Any piece of work is technically considered copyrighted when it is published, and that automatic copyright is recognized in most countries for 70 years from the date of publication.

However—and here's why it gets confusing—you must register the work at www.copyright.gov to obtain an official copyright in order to be able to sue someone engaged in copyright infringement. So if you find your book being pirated on some website after publication, you can only pursue legal action if the work is registered (registration fees start at $35; the process does not require any legal representation). Adding to the confusion is the fact that every country has different copyright laws—make sure you check the laws for your country of residence to see whether you need to register the work for protection in the territory you are selling it. But because Amazon (and almost all the other distribution networks) are based in the United States, you will need to register your work with the U.S. Copyright Office to get this protection, even if you are located elsewhere.

PRODUCING AN AUDIOBOOK

In the five years between 2013 and 2018, spending on audiobooks doubled. In June of 2018, the CEO of the Publisher's Association called it 'the fastest growing area of consumer publishing,'[3] and at the time of writing, in Quarter One 2019, a surprising number of brand-name authors are opting to produce their books exclusively in audio format. This shift is bringing a lot of innovation to the publishing industry, but most importantly for you, readers are flocking to the audio format in droves.

To produce an audiobook, you will need to decide if you are going to record it yourself or have some voice talent read it for you. Once recorded, each chapter will need to be uploaded to the publishing platform to ensure it meets their quality standards, and then the collection of chapters will be combined in order to be published. To that end, if you choose to narrate it yourself, it's worth booking yourself into a proper recording space to do it—sitting in your house and recording it into a piece of software is not going to produce the quality you need. Once it's recorded, you will need to work with an audio producer to ensure that all the levels are balanced and that there are no problems with the final files, which is obviously an additional expense.

If you have a professional voice actor record it, however, they will take care of all the production. There will still be the expense of paying for their time, but I would say that for most authors, this is the better option—particularly if you're not used to narrating, this can be very time-consuming and tedious. All that said, I think that producing an audio version is absolutely worth the cost—it makes your book accessible to a much wider audience, makes buyers much more likely to actually engage with the content (how many ebooks have you bought that are still sitting unread on your Kindle?) and is a subtle marker of credibility and authority, because it takes work and investment to produce that format.

❦ 8 ❦

LAUNCH AND MARKETING

In an ideal world, you would start marketing your book the day you start working on it. As soon as I start working on a new project with a client, it's one of the first things we talk about. Most of my projects take about three months, and in that time, a huge number of marketing opportunities can emerge—and if you're not thinking about it, you'll miss them. A lot of people think of marketing as the thing that you do at the end of the process, but if you only start marketing your book on the actual release date, you will launch to crickets. If nobody knows it's coming, there's no anticipation, there are no people eagerly waiting to get their copy and leave their review, we've just missed three months of opportunity.

BRING YOUR AUDIENCE WITH YOU

Most people who choose to write a book about their business already have some kind of established audience—say, a social media following, an email list, a private or members-only group, a buyers' list or a robust personal network. To ignore the value and opportunity in priming that audience for the launch of your book is a total waste of your previous marketing efforts to build that audience. It's actively shooting yourself in the foot for the success of your launch day and the ongoing marketing of your book.

Many soon-to-be-published authors have a lot of resistance to talking about a book that's not quite ready yet—either because they are perfectionists, or they want to keep all their powder dry for the actual launch period—but the people in your audience, who are already invested in you and your brand, *want* to know about this kind of project. They want to come along for the journey with you, and if you give them the opportunity to be involved throughout the whole process, it can create a huge groundswell of support. And believe me when I say, you cannot buy that kind of publicity. A vocal community of people who know, like and trust you, and who are personally invested in the success of your project, is the holy grail of launching a book, so involve your audience as much as you can, as soon as you can.

Before we get started on all the different types of marketing you can deploy to launch your book, I would like to include a few caveats. First, you do not have to implement all the marketing ideas that I am about to lay out. Focus on the channels where you are already doing really well; you do not have to generate strategies for platforms where you have no experience or inclination to spend your time. If you are killing it on YouTube but the thought of wrangling radio interviews makes you panic, just double down on YouTube. Or if you have an extremely engaged email list and you've never touched Facebook in your life, don't worry about switching—stick with what's already working. You can pick and choose what's going to work for you and your audience, particularly if you already know where your audience congregates. If you know they're not on Twitter or Instagram, don't bother spending your resources marketing to an empty space.

Second, all your marketing for the book does not have to happen as soon as you launch. Books are a somewhat unique product, in that they can keep selling steadily for *years* if the material is timeless and good quality. While a strong launch is certainly important, you can take a long view with it, and roll out marketing campaigns gradually, as you have the resources.

Paul Jarvis talked about both these caveats in his recap on launching his own book, *Company of One*:

> I fully burnt myself out during this process as I've been doing two to four interviews a day... It's so much work, and while enjoyable, it's completely draining to be "on" as an introvert. I thought I paced things well, but I should have done a better job with it. It's a marathon, not a sprint, to get word out. Books can last forever, so promotion doesn't have to happen all at once.
>
> It's worth mentioning that any/all promotion or publicity is optional. And as the author, you can say no to anything specific you either don't want to do or don't feel is right to do.[1]

BECOMING A BESTSELLER... OR NOT

A common goal among writers when they start thinking about marketing their book is to become a bestseller. Normally, this is because they want the book to sell well in its category, and to be able to use its bestseller status as marketing ammunition. Those are both sensible and respectable goals.

In fact, I think this is very much a goal you should aspire to, as evidenced by the subtitle for this book. But I am specifically talking about becoming a bestseller in your category or niche— outselling everyone else who has published a book in that niche for at least a brief interval.

The reason I make this distinction is that, like the whole ISBN thing, getting onto the famous bestseller lists is a racket. (Maybe you're starting to see why traditional publishing was so ripe for disruption by the self-publishing movement.)

The New York Times Bestseller list is, for all intents and purposes, the most famous, sought-after and respected bestseller list in the world. But while their list is *based* on sales data, it is an editorialized version of what's selling—the lists are compiled from a selection of data, from a selection of vendors and publishers around the U.S., but the *Times* is not required to present the actual facts of what is selling, so they can be selective about which books actually make it onto the lists.

I am not being snarky or conspiratorial here.

William Blatty, author of *The Exorcist*, sold so many copies of his second book, *Legion*, when it launched that by the numbers, he should have trounced every other book on the list. But *The New York Times* didn't include *Legion* on the list until many weeks later, with a lot of prompting, and then only for a week, when it should have stayed put for months. Blatty sued the paper in the early 1980s, arguing that the book's absence from the bestseller list had a material impact on its sales and that he had suffered financial damages as a result. He lost, and appealed all the way to the Supreme Court, where the case was dismissed, based on the *Times'* defence that "the list did not purport to be an objective compilation of information but instead was an editorial product."[2]

So while Batty had to soldier on, the *Times* was free to continue presenting its list free of consequence, since the Supreme Court had ruled that, since it was an editorial product, it was protected under the First Amendment's protection of free speech, and could not be used as grounds for legal action. The paper did eventually add a little fine print to note that "sales figures are statistically adjusted"—meaning that they take data from a select number of sources and extrapolate what they *believe* to be the bestsellers (or, if you're a cynic, they pick the books they deem worthy and make it so).

More recently, *The New York Times* released a statement describing how they curate their lists, and buried among all the self-congratulatory emphasis on how fair they are, there were a few buried gems like this (italics mine):

- "Institutional, special interest, group or bulk

purchases, if and when they are included *[in the data]*, are at the discretion of *The New York Times* Bestseller List Desk editors based on standards for inclusion that encompass proprietary vetting and audit protocols, corroborative reporting and other statistical determinations."

- "Free trial or low-cost audiobook sales are not eligible for inclusion."
- "Among the categories not actively tracked at this time are: *perennial sellers*, required classroom reading, textbooks, reference and test preparation guides, *e-books available exclusively from a single vendor*, journals, workbooks."[3]

In their huge *Book History (Volume 3)*, Ezra Greenspan and Jonathan Rose note:

The politics of the bestseller list is an issue that should concern both scholars of the book trade and those who look to the bestseller lists to provide useful information on people's reading habits. I do not mean to suggest here that existing bestseller lists bear absolutely no relation to actual sales of books. A title that appears on the *Times* list (or one of the other major lists) probably is selling in high numbers. But rankings may not always be deserved, and there may be other high-selling titles that do not make it onto the lists. Therefore, scholars *[or writers]* who want to use such lists as records of popular tastes need to scrutinize more closely the context in which they are produced. They should understand that *the authority of the list is more cultural than scientific, and that the purpose of the list is as much about economics as it is about entertaining or informing the public. While the bestseller list does not necessarily give us a transparent account of Americans' reading patterns, it can tell us a lot about the social production of bestsellers.* [4]

(Again, italics mine for emphasis.)

This selective reporting happens at all the major bestseller lists to some degree. To quote publisher Tucker Max, "Every single list is either measuring a limited number of sales in a few places, or far worse, it's a curated list and a small group of people are deciding what to put on their list. And they're picking books based on what they think are 'important' books, not based on what is actually selling... it's curated elitism."[5]

So there's that.

When it comes to hitting the bestseller list on Amazon, things are a bit different, and I suggest this is where you focus your attention. If you sell the most books in your category, you will be listed as the bestseller. This list is actual sales reporting, and it's updated hourly to give the most accurate picture of what's selling in each category.

While there's not specific information available on the details of the algorithm, if you sell a hundred books one hour and none the next, you won't drop off the list—you will just fall down a few spots in the top ten rank, if other titles in the category are still selling. It seems to be factoring in a time variable that compares you to other titles in the category (for example, if no one else has sold many copies recently, the short window of your sales seems to be weighted positively in influencing your spot in the results).

A very important note: Do not try to game Amazon. Do not buy lots of copies for yourself through the sales page. If you legitimately want copies, you can buy them at near-cost price through KDP. Do not, I repeat, *do not* try to engineer bestseller status by just buying a thousand copies. Amazon tracks IP addresses and credit card details very closely, and stories abound of authors trying to cheat the system, and instead having their book pulled from the platform and their account permanently banned. I beg you, don't do it.

(And please, for the love of all that is good in this world, stay away from those charlatans who promise to get you on the bestseller list for a fee. It's outrageously expensive, not at all guaranteed to work, and you are exposed to the very real risk of being banned from all the major sales platforms if the company gets caught.)

So yes, there's value in getting the title of bestseller. It definitely carries a lot of clout and influence in the minds of most consumers, and the best way to become a bestseller is to write a kick-ass book, get some genuine endorsements, and market the hell out of it. So without further ado, let's get into how to do that.

HOW TO MARKET YOUR BOOK

Pre-Order Campaigns

KDP allows you to run pre-order campaigns when you upload your book to the platform at least ten days in advance of the publication date. (That's the minimum; you can start a pre-order campaign months before if you're ready.) This can be a huge opportunity, because every pre-order counts as a sale on launch day, and the more sales you have on launch day, the higher your book will rank in the search results for the category and keywords you selected.

Amazon favors products that have a stable sales velocity—the rate at which the product is selling—so launching with a lot of pre-orders means that your sales velocity is more likely to stabilize at a higher volume than if you launched with no pre-sales, creating a virtuous cycle with Amazon's algorithm. More sales equals more visibility. More visibility equals more sales.

Podcast Tour

With the exception of authors with a particular skillset in one of the other areas of marketing listed here, I believe that a podcast tour is currently the most valuable place to spend most of your time and energy. Podcasts are incredibly popular, and have huge, engaged networks of listeners who are actively seeking content relevant to their interests. You get a lot of exposure for a relatively low time investment for each interview, and podcasts have a very long tail—they rank well for SEO, new listeners will often listen to a whole back-catalog to 'catch up' and come across your episode, and hosts will often bump old episodes as part of their own marketing cycles.

Go to iTunes and look at all the podcasts listed in the category relevant to you and start reaching out to them as soon as you start writing—many shows get a huge volume of pitches and so you will need to work out how to connect with the hosts and differentiate yourself from everyone else clamoring to get featured. You can gradually build up interactions with them through their email list or social media presence, leverage your six degrees of separation, or come up with something creative to send them.

Ask your audience about their favorite shows, and for introductions whenever possible. Lean on your personal network here too—if anyone hosts a show, or has a connection to one, then ask for their help.

When you do book an interview, make sure you're ready to capitalize on that opportunity. Set up a landing page with a URL that's unique to that podcast, and offer some kind of free giveaway to their audience. That way, you can collect email addresses, tag them in your email software with the referring source (which podcast they came from), so you can continue to market directly to them with tailored, relevant material as you come up to your launch.

It might seem counterintuitive, but this is also a good time to launch your own podcast, if you don't already have one. If you're recording interviews to produce the material, or if you're interviewing contributors, you're producing a lot of extra content, which could be used for at least one season of a podcast. That way, you have a bit more credibility when you are approaching other podcasters and you also have a bit of leverage, in that you can offer them a return interview on your own show.

PRIVATE COMMUNITY

You can build up a private community on any platform you like. For the sake of simplicity, I'm going to focus on Facebook groups here, but you can apply this logic to email lists, other social media platforms, or independent membership sites.

If you don't already have a private space where you interact with your audience, start building one today. Put this book down if you have to; you need to develop a channel where you can interact personally with your future readers. At the very least, make sure you start the group while you're still working on the draft so that you can get early buy-in from the people who fit your reader avatar, and get them to help you promote it when the time comes.

Name your group something simple and easy to recognize (you can even just re-use the name of your book), and invite people to join. This might be past and current customers, leads who went cold, and people you know personally with an interest in your topic. I suggest reaching out personally, but you can also invite people through email and social media campaigns.

Now, don't just go adding people without their consent— even if you know they're a perfect fit for reading your book, they still need to 'opt in' to engage with you. Just because you *can* automatically add people to Facebook groups doesn't mean you should. Getting permission can be as simple as sending them a quick message on Facebook like this:

> *"Hi Peter! I'm working on a book about how SMEs can get predictable results with their paid advertising campaigns, and I've started a private Facebook group to talk about it all with folks who are interested. I know you've been doing a lot of work to make your ads convert better—want to join us?"*

Invite people in your network who are interested and knowledgeable about the content you're covering, and can be trusted to give you honest feedback, to ask thought-provoking questions, to act as early readers, and to support you getting the book out into the world. You can also encourage each of those members to add people from their own networks who also fit this profile.

Having this early involvement gives people a sense of ownership in the book, so they will be more likely to help promote and share it with people in their own networks at the time of publication.

But don't forget that this has got to be a two-way street. They're helping you a lot with feedback on the material for the book, the title, cover and so on. Make sure you're providing them with value too—teaching them new stuff regularly, sharing cool resources, answering their questions and sharing ideas. Give them sneak peeks of the material you're working on (not the fluffy stuff—material they can actually start using right away) and be generous and engaged with them as often as possible.

EMAIL MARKETING

If you have an existing email list that you communicate with regularly, start seeding information about your book to them as soon as you start writing. Invite them to join your private group, too. While both are channels where they can interact with you directly, the benefit of joining the group is that they will also get to interact with other members—people who are most likely interested and experienced in similar things. It's a great way to start building up a community that isn't directly reliant on you, since members can build their own connections independently and expand their own network that way.

Regardless, since your email list already knows, likes and trusts you, they can be a great source of insight when you are building out the content. Send them a survey about the topics you are planning to write about, or ask them to vote for topics they would like you to cover. Make sure that anything interactive you do with them is tracked—set up your email campaign with tracked links so that you can segment your list according to who has engaged with your book material. When it comes time to launch, you can then send different campaigns to the people who engaged with the book process and those that didn't. This is simple best practice for sales campaigns—you need to tailor your messaging based on the previous actions of the audience.

If you are using the book's publicity as a way to grow your email list, make sure you have an autoresponder sequence set up that welcomes your new subscribers and familiarizes them with your business in a way that is congruent with what they first learned about you in the book. Make sure you're also tagging new subscribers in your email software with their referring source so you can continue to market to them with tailored, relevant material.

Social Media

As I said earlier, focus on the social media channels where you are already established and successful. If you know that your audience is using a platform that you have not yet focused on, then marketing your book there can be a great way to get started, but if you're already up and running, I strongly suggest just focusing your efforts where they are going to have the most impact.

In this section I am focusing on organic social media engagement; we'll talk about paid campaigns later. There are two elements to marketing your book on social media: posting your own content about the book, and orchestrating other people posting about it.

Your own strategy should be to create as much interest and value for your audience as possible, and to move them to an action: opting in to hear more about the book (in the pre-launch phase) or to buy it (in the launch phase). Depending on the engagement of your audience, you might need to lead them through a series of smaller commitments first (for example, the sequence might be *like this page > leave a comment > join our private group*, or *click here to read more > sign up here for a sample > buy the book*).

The type of content you post should be derived from or closely related to the book's main theme. If you can post videos with people you interviewed, or share quotes, or give away small, useful parts of the material, then people are going to be far more likely to engage than if you just post constantly that the book is out and they should go buy it. Prioritize giving your audience real value, making the launch process something that benefits them and increases their goodwill towards you—not something that drains that goodwill down to nothing.

In terms of managing other people posting for you: ask the people who have shown interest on email list and private group to commit to sharing something on social media when the book launches.

(This used to be very easy with a tool called Thunderclap, which basically pre-filled a post for them on their linked social media channels, scheduled the posts, and then posted them automatically on launch day. Sadly Facebook banned Thunderclap's integration and the service ceased to be viable, so now you have to do this manually.)

You can give people specific copy to post on a specific date, in order to remove the 'I don't know what to post' point of failure. Ask everyone you can think of to post for you—family, friends, colleagues, past clients, and anyone who gave you an endorsement. The more coverage you can generate organically, the better, and I'll delve a little more into this in the section on outreach to your personal network.

INFLUENCERS

If you have existing relationships with social media influencers, and your book is going to be relevant to them and their audience, by all means, try to have them promote it. If you are starting from scratch though, you might want to 'trade up the chain' a bit—get the book out in the world, get some credibility and buzz going, and *then* reach out to relevant influencers, so that they can see straight away that it will be worthwhile for them, rather than risking their brand equity on an unknown quantity.

CONTENT MARKETING

If you are already creating content regularly as a way of generating traffic and leads, then certainly use your book as a central theme of your content throughout the production and launch process. This is a great opportunity to invite people who are new to your audience to join your email list or private group —you can offer a sample of the book as an opt-in offer to get them across the line.

You can feature a few chapters of the book as blog posts, or share interviews with contributors as podcasts or videos. You can record yourself talking about particular topics and have it transcribed (and edited a little) as blog posts or email campaigns, or post them to your social media channels. Remember that content marketing is not just about writing blog posts. Any content that you develop with the intent to capture the attention and details of your audience counts.

Best practice, of course, is to promote your new content across each of your active channels. If you put a video up on YouTube, make sure you post about it on your other social channels, and share it with your email list. Much of the time, your audience members will only follow one of your channels, so they will miss out on your content if you don't promote it on their specific channel. And again, make sure you have a way to capture email addresses or memberships for your private group (a landing page, an opt-in box, or a link to your group). It doesn't have to be complicated, just make sure that you're actually capturing the attention that your content generates.

PERSONAL NETWORK OUTREACH

Your personal and professional networks are likely to be one of the most valuable resources at your disposal for launching and marketing your book. I am going to assume here that you have been diligent in investing in these networks over the course of your career so far, and that you have mutually beneficial and respectful relationships with all the people that will come to mind for you here.

Promoting your book is one of the few times that I would recommend leaning heavily on your network for launch support. This includes asking the more visible people for endorsements for the book (or introductions to people who could give you an endorsement—more on this at the end of this section), as these will have a significant impact on your credibility and will influence more skeptical readers to purchase. Other people will have large communities (on email or social media) that would be ideal readers, and others still are just great evangelists for products they feel strongly about.

If you are looking for an endorsement, reach out early—as soon as editing is done, so that the person you are approaching can read the material if they want to and have time to think about what they want to say. This is also around the time you should reach out if you are looking for a promotion to someone's list or audience—your contact will probably want to see the content in order to feel comfortable sharing it. And if you are just reaching out to ask someone to read the book or to share it, you can reach out when you are about to launch.

When I launched my first book, *Content That Converts*, I emailed everyone that I mentioned in the book the day before it went live. The emails were personalized variations of the following:

Hi [NAME],

How's it going? I hope everything with [THING] went well.

This email is just to let you know that I'm releasing a new book tomorrow, and I mentioned you in it. It's about content marketing, and your article about [RELEVANT THING] really helped me when I first started working on it.

The book will be available at [LINK] from tomorrow if you are interested in checking it out. If you like it, I would be really grateful for a review or a mention on social media (and no pressure at all if it's not a good fit for you).

Looking forward to catching up soon!

Laura.

You can also draft all these emails in advance and then send them on the day of the launch so that the link is live and they can just go straight to it. You can also create a variation for people you just think would be interested but weren't mentioned —just remove the line about their work, and replace it with something personal or interesting to them.

These emails went to everyone that I had worked with in the last couple of years, everybody in my friendship network, in my business network, everybody that I could justify reaching out to. I did it one by one, and that ended up being a huge element of why the book was successful—it was really personal, and the requests were carefully tailored to each person, based on the relationship I had with them. So even if you don't have a huge network or if you don't have a huge online presence, you can still make a lot of headway, just by personal connection and by asking your network to check it out.

This seems like a lot of heavy lifting, especially if you have a big network, but it is so worth it. People who know and like you are going to be excited that you've gone through this huge process and will be interested in seeing the result of your work (particularly if they are mentioned in it).

Not only that, but many of your contacts will not see your marketing, for whatever reason, and often they will be the most qualified prospects you have. If they are ideal readers, they are probably connected to many other people who are also ideal readers. Just make sure that you are providing as much benefit to them as you are hoping to receive in return—you don't want to drain your goodwill by making people feel used. If you are genuine and friendly, the relationship is in good condition and your material is good, there's no reason for people to turn you down.

GETTING ENDORSEMENTS AND REVIEWS

Endorsements, also referred to as book blurbs (often confused with the 'blurb' material on the back cover of the book, describing what the reader will find within) are one of the most powerful marketing tools at your disposal. Even a handful of endorsements from celebrities or industry authorities can catapult the book to the top of a bestseller list almost instantly.

A good endorsement lets a potential reader know that this book is going to be relevant to them, that you are a credible source of information, and that this book is important enough that the potential reader should buy it.

The point of an endorsement is that you get to borrow that person's credibility. Sometimes a person who is relatively unknown but holds a high-status position can give just as powerful an endorsement as someone who is famous. This opens up an extra line of people to think about—people in important positions in your industry, at well-known institutions and so on.

All that said, endorsements are not essential to launching and marketing your book. If getting endorsements is getting in the way of you doing the actual work of writing, editing or marketing your book, let it go. You can get endorsements later on and add them to your sales page or use them as a reason to reach out to your audience to promote the book again later on.

Reviews, on the other hand, *are* essential to marketing your book. Obviously you can't get reviews for your book prior to the launch date, but ask people—like your early readers, pre-order buyers and inner circle to buy the book on launch day and leave a review right away. The more reviews you can garner early on, the better—this also contributes to the weighting Amazon's search algorithm will give your book in the search rankings.

Ask people to leave reviews when they are logged into their account (these reviews are 'verified' which have higher credibility than anonymous reviews). While Amazon does not allow you to incentivize reviews, there's no reason you can't incentivize people off the platform—have people send you a screenshot of their published review in exchange for some kind of bonus.

People who are browsing Amazon will almost certainly go straight to the review section to determine if a book is worth their time. If there are very few reviews—or none—they will probably go back to browsing and try to find something that's a more proven success. But even a few enthusiastic early reviews can be enough to generate the critical mass that will make the sales velocity self-sustaining.

Finally, keep asking people for reviews as time goes on—the more you have, the better, and people coming across your book for the first time will be more encouraged to buy if there are recent reviews to look at (rather than reviews from, say, three years ago, since maybe other more relevant books have been published in the meantime).

PPC CAMPAIGNS

Pay-per-click advertising is another way you can get eyeballs on your offer in a reasonably reliable and predictable way. Molly Pittman (former Vice President of Digital Marketer, co-founder of Digital Strategy Bootcamps, and media buyer extraordinaire), was generous enough to share her thoughts on what goes into making a successful paid ad campaign. This is not about the 'button-clicking,' as she calls it—there are plenty of tutorials online for how to actually set up the technical part of a campaign —this is about the strategy you need to make your campaigns a success. Note that this section is quite involved, so you may need to come back to it a couple of times to absorb everything covered here.

There are five elements involved in any successful ad campaign. All of these elements work together to create a cohesive, 'sticky' experience for the customer, where they are getting clear messaging from you and have a consistent experience from the moment they first see your ad, through to buying whatever it is you've put in front of them. All five are important and you have to have each piece in place if you're going to build a reliable and replicable campaign. A lot of people get caught up in the tactical button-pressing side of media buying and while that's important, if you always go back to the basics and focus on these five things, you're going to have success.

ELEMENT #1: OFFER

An offer does not mean your product. Your *product* might be a cool piece of software, but your *offer* might be a free fourteen-day trial to encourage prospects to buy the product. People often run ads that declare that their product exists, but they're not really making an offer or giving their audience a reason to click.

Your offer is the destination that you are running traffic to from this ad, along with the reasoning as to why they should take action. Just because people see your ad, there's no guarantee they're going to take action on it—you have to consider whether you're running traffic to something that people really want. As simple as it sounds, the number one factor in any successful paid ad campaign is to make sure you're buying traffic to something your audience will actually want.

The kind of offer you make is certainly going to be business-specific, but a lot of what makes an offer successful is psychological. What is it about your offer that provides a transformation for the end user? How are you taking them from a 'before state' of being unhappy with something, to an 'after state' of happiness and satisfaction? The offer is the vehicle that takes them from the 'before state' to the 'after state.'

ELEMENT #2: COPY

Your copy is the articulation of *why* the offer is something that the market wants. The offer and copy go hand-in-hand. Once you know what you're going to offer, and what the hook is that will transform the end user, the copy just about writes itself. I really recommend making the copy as personable and actionable as possible, particularly on Facebook and the other social platforms.

The more personal you can be, the more people are going to respond to your ad, which means they'll engage more with your ad, which means your relevance score will increase (which means that your ad will be shown more often). A huge mistake that people make on ad platforms is that they try to be too professional. They're so rigid that their copy does not relate to the audience. It doesn't feel like a conversation, or like a post from a friend, and since these are social platforms, you really need to have that more human touch. People are used to scrolling through their newsfeeds to see content from their family, friends and colleagues—they're not there to look at ads from brands. If you can meet them where they are at mentally at the moment they see your ad, it will go a long way. Making your copy very personal, just like you were talking to a friend, works very well for most businesses. You want to touch on the pain point your product or service solves, and also offer a solution, which would be for the prospect to click and take action.

People often ask about length and style, and these are both variables you have to test. I've seen short, witty ads do very well, and I've seen heartfelt multi-paragraph ads work well too. It really depends on where the customers are at in their awareness of your brand. (And if you do go for longer copy, make sure your call to action isn't buried at under seven paragraphs of text—put it earlier, because most people won't make it that far.)

ELEMENT #3: CREATIVE

Creative is the ad copy, the video, the images, the GIFs—whatever visual elements you are using for your ads. There are lots of different ways you can present your ads, and this is where a lot of people get lazy. People create really bad-ass campaigns and then just slap a stock photo on there, or a picture of a cat, and it is such a waste! This is the element of the ad that is most going to catch people's attention. This is not just about making them stop—it's about catching their attention because this offer relates to them so powerfully. Using a picture of pretty people on the beach, or of a cat doing something funny—that might get people to stop, but it's not going to be a qualified click.

I really recommend putting a lot of research and thought into your creative before you launch your campaign, because this is one of your biggest opportunities. So many people are visual learners, so you really have to make the most out of your ad creative.

Your creative can say as much about your offer as your copy does, so when you're writing your copy, you also need to come up with a message that can be communicated through visuals as well. Whenever I'm thinking about creative, I take keywords from the ad copy or themes that I want to portray and type them into Google. Then I click the image tab to see what images are ranking at the top of the page, which shows me what people are clicking most often in relation to those words. (Google knows better than anyone what the visual representation of those words is going to be, because they're indexing the Internet—they know how many people have clicked on this specific image in relation to that specific search term). This is a good research process to start to get creative ideas for the visual representation of the transformation you're trying to articulate through the creative.

The execution of the ad creative is important too, and you have a few options here. You can either create them on your own—iPhone images work really well on social platforms, because they feel real. Professional photos can also work, but they look more like an ad—a few years ago I would've said you have to work with a designer because it needs to look high-end, but that's not as much the case anymore. You just need to be able to relate to your audience.

It is wise to work with a designer if you're having custom images made, but it's important to keep in mind that your designer is not a marketer. Your designer is trained to create beautiful images, so don't just send them a landing page and say, "Hey, create ads for this." You actually want to give them direction. And that's why it's so important that you as the marketer sets the strategy first. Do you want the creative to be personal photos or do you want them to be cartoons? What do you want them to portray? How do you want them to look from a style perspective? Those are all questions you should be answering for the designer so that they know what you're looking for from a marketing standpoint.

ELEMENT #4: TARGETING

This is another stage where people create awesome campaigns, but then get lazy at a critical moment. Targeting is so important, especially on Facebook. It's so important because you can build an awesome ad campaign with wonderful copy and creative and offer, but if you put it in front of the wrong people it's not going to work, because it wasn't built for them.

The really common mistake here is that people set their targeting too broadly. When you go to Facebook to set up an ad campaign, you target your ads based on interests, which are data points that Facebook has collected based on what people have shown interest in on their Facebook account. So if the company is selling yoga clothing, for example, most people would just go into the ad manager, type 'yoga' into the interest search bar and target the, say, 30 million people in the world who have shown an interest in yoga on Facebook. But that's not the best place to start because that's not the core, avid part of the market. There's a difference between someone who's done yoga a couple of times in their life and someone who does yoga every day. And which one of those people do you think is more likely to buy yoga products? It's probably the one that does yoga every day. So we want to reach the core part of the market, not just anyone that's ever shown interest. And so that's why you must do research. You have to take your best guess and start typing keywords into the interest search field to see what's available to help you niche down as far as possible.

In this example, maybe that's targeting people who like a specific style of yoga, or have shown interest in teacher training. Even if you *are* the avatar you are targeting, you still want to use this research process so that you can find as many interests as possible inside of Facebook to target and reach this core part of your market. What brands or authority figures does this market look up to? Where do they get their information? If you target based on those types of interest, you're going to come much closer than just targeting a single point of interest inside the ad platform. You want to get very specific and granular here, so that you end up with an audience size of between roughly half a million people and two and a half million people. This is big enough for the ad platform to optimize who the ad is being shown to, and not so big that there are too many people for the algorithm to target ad sets effectively.

ELEMENT #5: AD SCENT

Last but not least is the user experience of the ad, also known as ad scent. This is something that most media buyers don't think about—it's the relationship between the ads that you're running and the page that traffic is landing on, and how congruent that experience is for the end user throughout the whole sequence. You want to make sure that wherever you're sending traffic, that the landing page is congruent with the ad.

Think about how your ad and landing page are going to work together from a stranger's perspective, and make sure it's a seamless process for prospects to move through each next step. The reason people clicked is the transformation opportunity you showed them in the ad, and so you have to continue that message onto the next page to keep their attention.

Let's say, for example, that you're sending traffic to an opt-in page where you're asking people for their email address, and that 25 percent of the people that land on that page actually subscribe, with a cost per lead of $2. That means you're also losing 75 percent of that traffic. To optimize that campaign, most people would make changes to their traffic campaign, which is fair enough, but they forget to think about the page the user is landing on, and often this is actually where the problem lies. If, instead of changing the traffic source, they changed the on-page experience, they could feasibly double that opt-in rate and take it to 50 percent, and that cost per lead would immediately be cut in half and go down to a dollar—just because of changes that they made on the page.

The core part of ad scent comes from the idea that we all browse the Internet in a hub and spoke model—we're all searching for something. Even if you're on Facebook mindlessly scrolling, your brain is on a hunt, which is why you can suddenly realize 20 minutes have gone by without you noticing. It's because everything that you were doing was congruent—you weren't seeing anything unexpected, everything was very consistent. In that situation, it's only when there is a point of incongruency that you hit the back button or close the tab. So as a marketer, you want to make sure you are providing the best ad scent possible so that people continue to take the actions you're wanting them to take.

There are a few elements that you want to maintain consistency with. One is design—it's great if you can use similar imagery between your ad creative and your landing page. If you have a video, you can use that same video on the landing page. Or if there's a certain color scheme, or whatever you're using in terms of imagery in your ads, that should also carry over to your landing page.

The second is copy and messaging. Use very similar copy in your ads to what is on your landing page, because if someone starts to read and they align with your ad copy and they click over to the landing page and they see consistent messaging, they're going to continue forward. Often I just use copy in my ads that already exists in the content on the landing page we're sending traffic to.

And finally, your offer should be consistent! Don't try to 'bait-and-switch' people. So many times, I've seen a dentist offering free teeth-whitening in the ad, but when you click over to the landing page there's just an opt-in form with no mention of that offer. I've even seen Universal Studios do this. I saw an ad for a free four-day, three-night vacation with Universal Studios and I clicked over to the page and there were a ton of packages I could buy, but no mention of the deal that they had offered in the ad. That's really confusing and jarring for the user, and it's often mistakes like this that drive leads away.

Another reason ad scent is important is that advertising platforms like Facebook and Google Adwords are monitoring this—how many people click on this ad, and then how much time do they spend on the next page? How many of them exit or hit the back button very quickly? That shows Google or Facebook that even though the ad might have a high click-through rate, whatever experience the advertiser is providing on the next page is just not congruent, so the algorithm should dial down the reach this ad is getting. So ad scent is really important to maintain consistency. And this isn't just in media buying—consistency is key throughout marketing in general, so make sure you always step back and look at the bird's eye view of the entire customer experience when you're running campaigns.

TRADITIONAL PRESS FEATURES

Just like every other type of marketing that uses someone else's platform, traditional media—newspapers, magazines, radio, television—requires a lot of work to develop relationships with the right people. You can buy advertising, if you have big budgets, or you can try to get interviews and reviews through accessing journalists. If you're going to go down this path, do a ton of research. Find out who writes for which section of the paper. Locate the name of the radio show's producer. Get an introduction to the local news anchor. Build your relationships with the right people and demonstrate to them why your material is going to be valuable to them.

Again, I recommend starting with this once the edits are finished, because most journalists will want to read at least a little bit of the material before agreeing to anything. When you pitch them, give them three to five ideas for stories, and some polished headlines to go with each. Don't just pop up in their inbox and expect them to fall over themselves—go humbly and be as helpful as possible. Make their job easy, because they are fielding pitches from people just like you all day, every day.

This is another area where, like dealing with influencers, you might need to trade up the chain. Start small—get an interview at the tiny local radio station, TV channel or newspaper in your town or district, where there is little competition and a pressing need for interesting content. Once you've secured a couple of those, and maybe some digital coverage, you can go out a layer, to statewide media properties, and then from there to bigger and bigger properties. It's okay if you don't debut on national TV or the *Huffington Post*. Big properties are looking for credibility and evidence of your value, and if you can show them a wide range of features, they'll be far more receptive to featuring you.

Of course, if you want to swing for the fences, you can do that too. It does work every now and then, but you've got to do something pretty darn special. I have had success...

- Wrapping free copies up in special wrapping paper and attaching a little gift that was related to the book with a personalized note to the journalist.
- Inviting a handful of high-level journalists to private events with the author (where the author had established credibility already).
- Making personalized videos with the author to send to the journalist, explaining why they would be a good fit for a feature.

Don't do creepy things like turning up at their office or bombarding them with dozens of calls or emails—play it cool. Media is a game, so see how creative you can get and how much fun you can have while playing.

Marketing is an inherently creative and innovative field. How you choose to promote and share your book with your audience is entirely up to you. You can do all of this, or none of it. You can take what works, leave what doesn't, and experiment with the ideas and strategies that are uniquely yours. Ultimately, what matters is that your book gets in the hands of the people you wrote it for. If that means that you just buy copies (through the correct channels, pretty please) to give out for free at speaking engagements and events, that's perfectly fine. If you orchestrate a multi-stage launch that blitzes every platform and throws in an international book tour to boot, more power to you. Do what's right for you, your book and your readers.

𝕏 9 𝕏

WHAT'S NEXT?

AT THIS POINT, YOU HAVE ABSORBED *A LOT* OF INFORMATION about how to write, edit, publish and market your book. We got into a lot of detail, so don't worry if you need to come back to it a few times to find what you need as you move through the process. Writing a book is a long process, and it can take a few attempts to get the final product across the finish line.

Once your book is out in the world, you can breathe a sigh of relief and take a step back from the project. Once your marketing campaigns are rolling, let your focus shift to something else for a while. This will give your mind some time to relax and start to come up with more creative ideas for how you can put the book to use in the future. There are so many ways you can make the book work for you, and I encourage you to experiment and make the most of the amazing asset you've built for yourself.

In the next section, you'll find case studies from clients I've worked with to write, edit, publish and/or market their books. These projects were all very different from each other, and the purpose and use of the books within each business have also been very different. They all had different questions and challenges throughout the process, which they share in their interviews, and I hope you'll find some inspiration in their stories. But first, there are a few parting thoughts I would like to leave you with on the process of writing a book.

One: This process belongs to you. Writing a book—even a business book—is an intensely personal experience and you should protect it from criticism (even the constructive kind) until you're confident that you've got a handle on the material. Having early readers is extremely valuable, but wait until you have a completed draft before you hand it out—don't let outside influences puncture your enthusiasm or derail you before you've made meaningful progress. You should also know that often it can be an emotional experience to review your history with the business. For a lot of entrepreneurs and business owners, building their company is the hardest, most demanding thing they've ever done, and much sacrifice has gone into it. If you find yourself feeling raw or overwhelmed, it's okay. Step away from the writing for a while to take care of yourself, and come back once you've let yourself process that past experience.

Two: the timeline and process here are a very reliable framework, but they are not the only framework. Sometimes there will be extenuating circumstances, or an opportunity will come up, or for one reason or another, you will just struggle with the next step in the process. That's okay too. If you need to tackle a step out of sequence, it's not going to blow up the whole project. Make sure you come back and fill in the gap later, but don't let the book stall or get completely sidetracked because you're trying to stick to the letter of my process.

Three: While this is going to be hard, it should also be fun. Writing is an incredible opportunity to get to know yourself and your own thoughts in a much clearer way than many people ever do. Various clients have told me that it was the first time they had articulated everything they know about their business and industry, and that it's both empowering and edifying to realize that you *are* in fact a true expert. Let yourself enjoy that, and make sure that you mark milestones along the way—finishing the draft, signing off on editing and so on—and when the book is finally published, have a launch celebration. Maybe that's a nice dinner with your family, or a full-blown launch party with family, friends, customers and partners in attendance. Mark the occasion, because publishing a book is a huge achievement, and you deserve to celebrate with the people in your life who make it all worthwhile.

Thank you for reading this book. I hope you've learned everything you were hoping to find, and that you're ready to go ahead and write a book that's going to be a powerful ambassador for your business out in the world.

If you're ready to get started, I'd like to invite you to go to www.lauraiswriting.com/workbook to download a workbook of exercises that will get you started on your own book project. You will also find additional resources and material on that page that will supplement what you've read here.

(You're also welcome to join the private Content That Converts Facebook group if you'd like to ask questions and meet people who are also writing and creating content, and if you want to be in touch to explore working together on a book, please go to www.lauraiswriting.com/services.)

Thanks again for reading *How To Write This Book*. Good luck with your project, and happy writing.

❧ I ❧
CASE STUDIES &
READING LIST

KIRI MASTERS, BOBSLED MARKETING

AUTHOR OF *THE AMAZON EXPANSION PLAN: LEARN HOW TO SKYROCKET YOUR SALES, SELL GLOBALLY AND MAKE YOUR BRAND AN INTERNATIONAL SUCCESS.*

WHAT WAS YOUR MOTIVATION FOR WRITING YOUR BOOK?

My agency focuses on serving larger, established companies who are selling on Amazon, and a lot of the content in our industry—in blog posts, podcasts and in other books—is focused on individual traders and entrepreneurs. There was a wide space in that field to talk to bigger companies, addressing sales teams and CMOs—I knew that if I could come in with an authoritative piece, it would create a lot of visibility and powerful positioning for us in the eyes of those companies. I had always done a lot of blog writing and other digital content creation, but a book seemed like a more legitimate business card to have.

HOW HAVE YOU PUT THE BOOK TO USE WITHIN YOUR BUSINESS?

We talk about it in our sales materials extensively. We get a steady, well-qualified stream of prospects from the book, and those prospects end up converting really well—if they end up contacting us after reading the book, it's because they really understand what we do, they agree with our methodology, they resonate with me personally, and they get the value of working with our company specifically, because they've already established a relationship with us through the book.

WAS THERE A PART OF WORKING ON THE BOOK TOGETHER THAT YOU PARTICULARLY ENJOYED?

The interviews were a really great way to crystallize how much you actually know about your field. There's so much that you don't even think about; it's not until somebody asks you about how something works, or why something is set up a particular way that you realize that what you know is not everyday knowledge for most people, even if they work in the same field.

WHAT WAS CHALLENGING THROUGHOUT THE PROCESS?

Doing the launch. It became so much bigger than I had expected. It was really worthwhile but it ended up becoming a huge campaign that took a lot of time and attention. Whenever I talk to people about writing a book I always say that they need to get help with at least one half of the process. So even though Laura took care of the actual production, I was still involved heavily in the launch process with my team, and there's no way I could have handled both elements and still run everything in the business every day—I could do one or the other; both would have been impossible. Another thing to keep in mind is that you really need to start the marketing as soon as you start work on the book too, even if that's just taking selfies while you're working on it to share on social media, starting to talk about it in blog posts and podcasts or whatever your main content platform is, so that when it gets to launch day there's already momentum and you're not trying to generate interest from scratch.

HAVE THERE BEEN ANY UNEXPECTED OUTCOMES OR OPPORTUNITIES THAT HAVE EMERGED AS A RESULT OF WRITING YOUR BOOK?

I had been blogging for a while, for my own site and for some other industry blogs, but when I wrote the book I felt confident to reach out to some bigger platforms to see if I could become a contributor. Having the whole package—the history of writing as well as all the authority of having written a successful book—boosted my credibility and visibility enough that I ended up becoming a contributor to Forbes. If you're trying to be a thought leader, it's really powerful.

WOULD YOU RECOMMEND WRITING A BOOK TO PEOPLE WHO ARE EXPLORING WAYS TO GROW THEIR BUSINESS?

You need to have a proven service or product offering that is going to allow you to capitalize on the authority that you're building through writing the book. If you have something you don't really know how to sell yet, or that you're not confident in, it's probably not the right play, but if you're confident in what you're selling and you know you can handle more leads and customers, then you should definitely consider it. It's much simpler than people realize to self-publish, and the credibility of being able to get a physical book into someone's hands, has been really valuable. It's really easy to do both ebook and physical formats, and it means you can use it for sales, for direct mail, for speaking events, there are so many benefits. It also gives you an opportunity to downsell to anyone you come across who's not a good fit for your product or service at the time—it's a really low-level commitment for someone to engage with you, so you're still getting your brand and approach out there, making a little bit of revenue from it, and getting someone into your ecosystem who might not be able to afford your services or isn't a good fit for you right now.

JEFF ROOT, SELLTERMLIFE.COM

AUTHOR OF *THE DIGITAL LIFE INSURANCE AGENT: HOW TO MARKET LIFE INSURANCE ONLINE AND SELL OVER THE PHONE.*

WHAT WAS YOUR MOTIVATION FOR WRITING YOUR BOOK?

There wasn't information online in one place that tackled the transition necessary for life insurance agents to move their businesses online. There's a lot to it—much more than I could have put in a blog post or even a series of blog posts—it really need to be presented in a cohesive way that presented all the information together, in context. I was doing a lot of training with agents and they all had the same questions, over and over, so I figured that the answers to those questions would make a great chapter structure for a book. There wasn't anything tangible that would teach agents to evolve and develop the skills they all need to keep moving into the future, so it was easy for me to see the benefit being the one to create that for our industry.

HOW HAVE YOU USED THE BOOK TO GROW YOUR BUSINESS?

I've had it on Amazon exclusively, but every time I speak at events, I bring copies of the book for all the attendees. I put it in my email signature, on my About page, everywhere I publish content that I'm the author of *The Digital Life Insurance Agent*, and it's done so much for my credibility. Most everybody I talk to for sales calls say that they've read my book, so people have a tangible sense of who I am and what I do. It makes doing business with them so much easier, because this book has been sitting on their desk or bookshelf staring at them until they're ready to act. It's easy to do business with someone when you've already demonstrated your knowledge to them, and having a book shortcuts the timeline of building a relationship with your prospects. Sales is all about rapport, and I've already built that rapport with them through the book.

HAVE THERE BEEN ANY UNEXPECTED OUTCOMES FOR YOU AS A RESULT OF WRITING THIS BOOK?

First of all, I'm still selling several copies every day, even though the book came out three years ago. I did not expect to be ranking on Amazon for this content for so long, and I didn't expect to get the speaking engagements I've been offered either. It's not exclusively because of the book, but it definitely has a lot to do with it—organizers always mention it when they invite me and it's always in the bios they put together for me. Honestly, it's one of the best decisions I've made for my business. It's been such a credibility builder and I've had a lot of opportunities because of it.

HOW HAS IT IMPACTED YOUR SALES?

I've had an increase in both the number of leads, and in how qualified those leads are too. In the business I run right now, almost all my customers have read my book, and often it's how they came across us in the first place. We've never paid for an ad to generate business, it's all been word of mouth referrals and people reading my book or listening to my podcast. Again, we published the book three years ago, and it hasn't slipped. I thought it would be dated or that people would discount it because they see a 2016 publication date, but that's not true. They're still buying it, still referencing it, still acknowledging it in the sales we do today. I thought I'd have to produce some other big asset by now, but the book is still giving people so much value that I haven't had to.

WAS THERE AN ELEMENT OF PRODUCING THE BOOK TOGETHER THAT YOU PARTICULARLY ENJOYED?

I enjoyed watching it come together. It was great seeing my thoughts go down on paper in a more cohesive, more organized way than I would have been able to do on my own. One thing that was a challenge was I didn't want to miss anything, so it was great getting on calls and then being able to look back over everything we talked about and plug in anything that I had forgotten or not explained enough, so that it was really thorough. In the end I felt confident that I didn't miss anything, because I'd had the opportunity to go through it in such a methodical way.

WHO WOULD YOU RECOMMEND WRITES A BOOK ABOUT THEIR BUSINESS?

If you know a lot about something, and people are tapping you for that knowledge regularly, then I absolutely recommend it. The main reason I did this book was to be able to teach more and to be able to cut down repeating the same things over and over. It's great in a situation where you want to be the authority, or people are always asking the same questions, but it's not right for everybody. For example, I work with life insurance agents, and I would not recommend they write a book—they don't have an audience that's going to read it, no one wants to read about life insurance if you're just trying to buy a policy—but from a business owner's perspective, if you have specific knowledge that you want to teach or get out into your industry then I do think it's really valuable.

IS THERE ANYTHING ELSE YOU WOULD TELL PEOPLE WHO ARE THINKING ABOUT WRITING A BOOK?

Don't be scared of a ghostwriter! And I'm not just saying that because Laura and I worked together; I'm totally serious. I was worried how the book would turn out when I first had the idea, but having someone there to help me who knew what they were doing meant that it all turned out perfectly.

RUSS PERRY, DESIGN PICKLE AND THE CREATIVE SYNDICATE

AUTHOR OF *THE SOBER ENTREPRENEUR* AND *THE CREATIVE ENTREPRENEUR*.

WHAT MOTIVATED YOU TO WRITE YOUR TWO BOOKS?

I had two very different motivations. The first book, *The Sober Entrepreneur*, was to create an asset for my family that was a collection of lessons learned from my own mistakes. I wanted to help them understand where I had come from and how we've come to where we're at now. Then I realized that those lessons didn't just have to be limited to my family, and that this story about isolation and addiction is so common among entrepreneurs, that I knew I could help a lot more people.

After that book was published though, I realized that even though it had gone out beyond my own little circle, I had still been focused on a very narrow audience (my family would only care about the personal stuff, and my audience would only care about the business stuff), so I wanted to write something else that was more universally applicable. For the second book, *The Creative Entrepreneur*, I wanted to give people a supplement to the systems I'd used to transform my life and business—a way they could customize those lessons to apply specifically to their own situation.

HOW ARE YOU USING THE BOOKS TO GROW YOUR BUSINESSES?

Both these books are designed to be lead generation tools for people who are interested in my cause or mission. The first book is about helping people to help themselves, and the second book is more specific to people within the creative business space, which our training and consulting company can really help them with. *The Sober Entrepreneur* was a phenomenal lead generation tool, and we basically had to create a new company to deal with all those leads, because people wanted help with stuff that was outside of what we were doing with Design Pickle. So *The Creative Entrepreneur* is a clear entry-point to what we're doing in the new company, The Creative Syndicate. It's still a stand-alone piece of content—I'm not teaching 10 percent of the material and trying to push them into my community to get the rest, they get it all up front—so the reader could change their whole life and business on their own.

Most people do better with accountability and coaching, so our offer is a natural extension to the book, but having them read it first acts as a filter to qualify if they're a good fit for what we're doing. We're about helping people to change themselves for the better, so if they're not willing to read a book and do some exercises there, they're probably not a good fit for our program, but if they are willing to do that and they resonate with what I'm teaching, then they're already on the road to transformation and I know they're more likely to be teachable and motivated.

WHICH PART OF THE PRODUCTION PROCESS HAVE YOU ENJOYED THE MOST?

The conversations where Laura interviews me for the material. I love what comes out of those calls, because I could never predict what I will end up saying. Her way of navigating my expertise and extracting deep information is really valuable, and I always go away with new ideas and new ways to think about things that I would never have come up with on my own. I'm benefitting from the process as much as the reader is.

WHICH PARTS ARE CHALLENGING?

My schedule! When you don't have time to do the writing yourself, having a writer to help you is the only option, but even then I always underestimate how much time and attention I'm going to put into this. This kind of project is so powerful and so significant, so you do have to be able to prioritize it and carve out time to put your energy and attention into it. It's not painful at all—like I said, I love doing it, and once I get the calls on the schedule and actually show up, it's fantastic—but it's the type of work that falls into the 'Important, Not Urgent' quadrant of time management.

HAVE THERE BEEN ANY UNEXPECTED OUTCOMES FOR YOU FROM WRITING THESE BOOKS?

It's not a surprise, per se, but even two years later, I still get messages every single day about how *The Sober Entrepreneur* has changed peoples' lives. I hoped that the vulnerability and honesty would create that kind of reaction, but you can never know how something will be received, so the fact that it has had such an impact for people is very moving for me. I'll continue to pump dollars into promoting it in perpetuity, because it's timeless content and there are still so many people out there who need help.

WHAT WOULD YOU TELL PEOPLE WHO ARE THINKING ABOUT WRITING A BOOK?

This process is not for the faint of heart, but it's also proven to make an impact. It's a really exciting opportunity for sophisticated business owners who want to put something real and powerful out into the world. This isn't a voice-to-transcript stream of consciousness project—if they just want a cheapo lead generation tool with a catchy title that people can download as a PDF on their website, they should do that themselves or use one of the other content platforms out there. It might get the job done, but if their book is going to be significant and make a meaningful change in their life and business, they can't afford for it to be like all the other shit that's out there.

On my own, I could never produce something with the

clarity and ease of reading, the simplicity and completeness of the books that Laura produces. I love working with her and seeing what she creates out of my stories, because it's both a legitimate book in its own right, but it can also be used for all kinds of business purposes.

BRIAN KURTZ, TITANS MARKETING

AUTHOR OF *OVERDELIVER: BUILD A BUSINESS FOR A LIFETIME PLAYING THE LONG GAME IN DIRECT RESPONSE MARKETING.*

WHAT MOTIVATED YOU TO WRITE YOUR BOOK?

I believe that if you've 'done it', you have a responsibility to teach it. Having spent nearly forty years accumulating this knowledge, and working with mentors like Marty Edelston, Gene Schwartz, Gary Bencivenga and Jay Abraham, I felt like I had a huge responsibility to teach what I've learned to the next generation of marketers. I'm still adding to that knowledge, still learning, but I knew I could be the messenger to a lot of people who haven't learned about these critical concepts or who needed to hear them again in a new way.

I don't want to be the old-timer telling war stories, but I do want to teach people that if they can build their marketing based on some fundamental concepts, they'll really maximize their impact and improve what they're already doing well. I get incredible satisfaction in being the messenger that helps a new generation of marketers have those lightbulb moments that give them a huge leap forward. Having a book makes it so easy to do that and gives me a reason to be in touch with that whole audience.

WHICH PART OF THE PROCESS OF WRITING THE BOOK TOGETHER DID YOU FIND MOST SATISFYING?

Finishing it! Seriously though, early on, defining what the ten chapters were going to be gave me a lot more confidence. We started out with all this disparate information, I had dozens of blog posts that I wanted to include as material and a lot of material that I had already drafted. I remember the day Laura and I went through about a hundred blog posts and sorted them into themes, and that was such a great process. To take all my thinking and ideas, all the content I hadn't fully fleshed out, and sorting it into useful information was so satisfying. It was creating order out of chaos. Watching it take shape from a pile of blog posts, then a Word document, then an editing document, then the proof documents and finally into the hardcover—watching that metamorphosis was so powerful for me.

WHICH PART DID YOU FIND MOST CHALLENGING?

Knowing that there was always more I could do with it. I had to accept that there were things that wouldn't make the final cut, and that there were things I could have done more with, but eventually you just have to pull the trigger and send it out. Working with a writer/editor really helped. Laura worked so hard to capture my voice in everything she worked on, but editing was still so hard, and I only got through that because we had built such a strong foundation. But getting to the end of that process was really satisfying and well worth it.

WHAT WERE SOME UNEXPECTED OUTCOMES OF WRITING THIS BOOK FOR YOU?

I've never been shy, but the book has made me bolder. Asking to get on stages and to teach more has gotten a lot easier now that I've got the book as proof. The other thing that surprised me was the power of the 'further reading' list. I'm a slow reader, but over forty years there have been many books that influenced me, and so it was really interesting to have an opportunity to collate all those into one place. It wasn't just books about marketing—I have *Oh, The Places You'll Go* by Dr. Seuss, *The Alchemist* by Paulo Coelho, *Give and Take* by Adam Grant—and so now that list is an incredible resource. When I'm teaching, I have this really nice by-product I can direct people to when they need more help. It's a gift I can give people. The notes from the end of each chapter also mean that it's easy for me to create keynote speeches just by repurposing that material, so it's given me a lot more assets than I expected to get out of it.

And finally, getting the endorsements. I had written a book before, so I knew people would do it, but this one is my opus, and it's been so humbling and almost embarrassing sometimes to hear how kind and enthusiastic people have been about this project. Some of the endorsements brought me to tears—Dan Kennedy saying that David Ogilvy would applaud my work, and Mark Ford saying that I was the only person who could tell this story and teach these lessons. I didn't think that people would hate it or say mean things, but the degree of support and interest was incredibly gratifying.

WHY DID YOU DECIDE TO WORK WITH A TRADITIONAL PUBLISHER OVER SELF-PUBLISHING?

The beauty of self-publishing is that you control the work completely. You can print at very inexpensive prices, you can use the book however you want as part of any kind of marketing funnel—you keep all the cards and can do what you want, on your own timelines. For me, what is missing is what I call the friends and relatives factor. I didn't think this would influence me so much, but it did in the end. My mother is 93—she's not shopping on Amazon, so she's not going to see my book anywhere. With a traditional publisher, you get that more traditional distribution, where maybe the book is in airports, it's in your local bookstore, you get the satisfaction of the book having a physical presence out in the world for people to see.

It added also a legitimacy to this project for me, since I don't know if I'll write another one. This was my opus, my life's work —I wasn't just trying to get the minimum viable product out the door for lead generation, so I wanted to go all out. Being published by Hay House specifically made all the difference to me here, because they are a company that really understands direct response. I wouldn't have gone with another traditional publisher, because having that marketing mindset and understanding what I would want to do with it meant that we had congruence and consistency in how both parties wanted to launch and market the book. Hay House is the leading publisher of personal development books in the world, so when they launched their new business imprint, I got to be one of the first books they published in that space, and that felt like a really cool opportunity.

WHAT WOULD YOU ADVISE PEOPLE WHO ARE THINKING ABOUT WRITING A BOOK ABOUT THEIR BUSINESS?

Writing a book gives people in your audience a chance to resonate with you and your message, to become part of your world when the time is right for them and they're ready to act on what you have to say. It's an opportunity for you to be in front of them at that moment, when they most want and need your help. I know some experts who teach that having a book is the most important thing you can do for your business and your audience —create a book and your credibility skyrockets. Sending a signed copy with a personal note to people is an incredible entry point for them into your world—they come into your orbit really knowing who you are, what your values are, what you represent. At its core, it's about list building, about reach, and that translates to dollars and opportunities. I don't know of anything that could be better. It's the best way to build a business.

READING LIST

In this section I share my favorite books on the art and science of both writing and marketing. This is by no means an exhaustive list. As with most things, too much information can be as problematic as too little, and I would rather share a small selection that helps you move forward in a meaningful way, rather than dump dozens of recommendations on you that leave you overwhelmed. The books listed here are personal favorites that I read regularly and refer to in order to improve my own work. I think will give you the most bang for your buck, in terms of the time and attention you spend reading them, and in the value they will bring to your work.

WRITING BOOKS

On Writing Well: The Classic Guide to Writing Non-Fiction, by William Zinsser.

If you never read another book about writing, *On Writing Well* would be enough. It has been in print since 1976, and has sold well over a million copies, with very good reason. Zinsser's style is so approachable—it's like having your own personal writing teacher bending over your shoulder, giving you encouragement and coaching at every stage. I have this in both print and digital formats and still come back to it regularly.

ON WRITING: A MEMOIR OF THE CRAFT, BY STEPHEN KING.

This is a master class in the process of writing and a fascinating look behind the scenes onto one of the most prolific writers of our time. King is funny and pragmatic—reading his advice on the technical aspects of writing is both incredibly informative and a bit like being heckled by a childhood friend. Very useful and a lot of fun.

THE FOREST FOR THE TREES: AN EDITOR'S ADVICE TO WRITERS, BY BETSY LERNER.

Lerner worked in New York publishing houses for many years, and worked with every type of writer and book imaginable. Her commentary on the process of writing, the power of editing, and the state of the publishing world is illuminating. If you're interested in pursuing a traditional book deal, Part Two of this book deals with publishing and is very informative.

WRITING DOWN THE BONES: FREEING THE WRITER WITHIN, BY NATALIE GOLDBERG.

This book has made me fall in love with writing, over and over again. It gives you permission to write in the way that's natural to you, instead of trying to hold you to someone else's process. It teaches you how to make a start, even if you believe right now that you could never write a single word that anyone else would want to read. Goldberg is a marvellous teacher, who loves her subject and her students, and *Writing Down The Bones* is both a roadmap and a joy to read.

PERFECT ENGLISH GRAMMAR: THE INDISPENSABLE GUIDE TO EXCELLENT WRITING AND SPEAKING, BY GRANT BARRETT.

Even though I did several units on grammar during my

writing degree, there is just no way I can remember all the tiny, finicky details of the English language. When I'm in flow and actually writing good material, the last thing I want is to get held up fretting about whether I'm writing date formats correctly or whether I should be using an en dash or an em dash. This book makes it really easy to check all those little details you're unsure about once you get to the editing stage.

MARKETING BOOKS

SCIENTIFIC ADVERTISING, BY CLAUDE HOPKINS.

This was the first book I ever read about marketing, and it gave me a very firm foundation to build my career on. It cleared away all the mystique around marketing and showed me how to think about campaigns holistically and with the right metrics in mind.

BREAKTHROUGH ADVERTISING, BY EUGENE M. SCHWARTZ.

This book is a master class in marketing. It delves deep into understanding your market, crafting effective offers and copy and the various sales mechanisms that you can use in any kind of campaign. It's very dense but will yield new ideas and insights on every reading.

OVERDELIVER: BUILD A BUSINESS FOR A LIFETIME PLAYING THE LONG GAME IN DIRECT RESPONSE MARKETING, BY BRIAN KURTZ.

In all transparency, I worked with Brian on this book as a developmental editor, but I honestly believe it is the practical compendium to *Breakthrough Advertising*. *Overdeliver* teaches all the critical business elements of marketing—understanding the principle of Recency, Frequency and Monetary scoring, controlling your costs to acquire customers, maximizing customer lifetime value, using predictive modelling to forecast revenues and profits, and most importantly, building relationships with customers that will allow you to run a sustainable, profitable business for many years.

No B.S. Marketing To the Affluent, by Dan Kennedy.

Don't let the title fool you; this book is about marketing to *any* highly motivated audience. Kennedy's point is all about picking a market that wants what you have, and has the resources to pay what you ask for it. It's a playbook in understanding the psychology of sophisticated markets and maximizing your ability to connect with them.

80/20 Sales and Marketing, by Perry Marshall.

I can't emphasize enough how powerful Marshall's book has been for me. Focusing on the 20 percent of work that yields 80 percent of the results? That's a priceless skill and will hone your marketing focus down to very targeted offers and audiences, in turn saving you from wasting time and resources on campaigns that don't grow your business.

NOTES

INTRODUCTION

1. http://timconley.co/are-you-really-ready-to-scale/
2. https://tim.blog/2016/11/21/tools-of-titans-derek-sivers-distilled/

1. DEFINING THE PURPOSE OF YOUR BOOK

1. https://www.mpg.de/596269/pressRelease200908171
2. Drucker, P., in Hotler, P., *Standing Room Only: Strategies for Marketing The Performing Arts*, Harvard Business Press, 1997.
3. https://www.briankurtz.me/when-i-stop-talking-youll-know-im-dead/
4. https://www.perrymarshall.com/adwords

2. DEFINING YOUR READER

1. https://www.digitalmarketer.com/blog/customer-avatar-worksheet/
2. https://hbr.org/2014/03/choosing-the-right-customer
3. Schwartz, E., *Breakthrough Advertising*, Titans Marketing, 1966.

4. WRITING YOUR DRAFT

1. https://www.amazon.com/Deep-Work-Focused-Success-Distracted/dp/1455586692
2. Lerner, B., *The Forest For The Trees: An Editor's Advice To Writers,* Riverhead Books, 2000.
3. Brown, S., Vaughan, C., *Play: How it Shapes the Brain, Opens the Imagination, and Invigorates the Soul,* Avery.

5. EDITING

1. From the speech, "Citizenship In A Republic," Paris, France, April 1910.
2. King, S., *On Writing: A Memoir of the Craft,* Scribner, 2000.

7. TYPESETTING AND PUBLICATION

1. http://www.bowker.com/products/ISBN-US.html
2. https://www.merriam-webster.com/dictionary/copyright
3. https://www.theguardian.com/uk-news/2018/jun/09/audiobooks-audible-publishing-sales-boost

8. LAUNCH AND MARKETING

1. https://pjrvs.com/launch/
2. Rose, E., Rose, J., *Book History, Vol. 3: 2000*, Penn State University Press.
3. https://www.nytimes.com/books/best-sellers/methodology/
4. https://www.amazon.com/Book-History-Vol-3-2000/dp/0271020504
5. https://scribewriting.com/get-best-seller-list/

ACKNOWLEDGMENTS

This book is only possible because so many people have trusted me to hone my process on their projects, and that is both a huge responsibility and an honor. For that I am hugely grateful to my clients: Brian Kurtz, Kiri Masters, Jeff Root, Russ Perry, Molly Pittman, Marcella Allison, Bob Cooper Jr., Tim Conley, Amanda Wells, Maneesh Shah, Michaela Light, Taylor Pearson, and all the copy and content clients before them that gave me the reps necessary to write at this level.

I'm also endlessly grateful for the constant love, courage and intellectual pushing I receive from many people in my personal life, which enables me to bring all my focus and energy to this work. Huge love and thanks to Molly Pittman, Lindsay Marder, Rachel Mazza, Laura Hietala, Alexis Shields, Elise McKenzie, Rosie Moore, Rory Dyck, Lauren Matthews Martins, Maria Rantanen, Michael Cecchin, Jack Benton, Sam Lehr, Leah Johns, Jodi Ettenberg, Christian Grattan, Matt McGrail, Elisa Doucette, Eric Bakey, Ando McCall, Rog Lawson, Frederico Catarino, Idahosa Ness, Branko Mijatovic, Aaron Evans-Agoghbe, Holly Dolke, Ayman Al-Abdullah, and of course, Mum & Dad, Jess, Em, Sashy and the rest of my lovely family.

To Brad Robinson—thank you for being an early reader and

for your ideas and feedback, and to everyone in the Content That Converts Facebook group, for your support, enthusiasm and patience.

A big shout-out to Ashlee Berghof and her team at A Squared Process Design, who keep me sane, on-task and making progress in my own business. Also Kat Cox, for helping me so much in producing additional content and bonus material for this book.

A not-insignificant part of this book happened due to the good people of Lisbon who keep me caffeinated, fed and properly socialized: Thaís & the gang at Copenhagen Alcântara, the crew at Mercearia da Mila, Rhi & Agne at Café Dede's, and João, Bruno & their team at Mercearia de Campo de Ourique.

I want to make a special mention of Brian Kurtz, who has taught me more than anyone about the principles and mechanics of marketing, and who has been generous and helpful beyond all measure. Another special mention to Marcella Allison, who has been a shining example of good cheer under pressure, and who could teach a master class in showing up—her presence, willingness to get real and vulnerable, and endless empathy and insight have been such a powerful example for me.

Finally, to you—I am acutely aware of what a privilege it is to teach you. I'm grateful and humbled by your interest in this work, and look forward to connecting with you when the time is right.

Made in the
USA
Lexington, KY